Morgan Harper

BARILOCHE

TRAVEL GUIDE 2025

A TRAVELER'S GUIDE TO OUTDOOR
ADVENTURES, HIDDEN GEMS, AND LOCAL
CULTURE IN BARILOCHE, ARGENTINA

Bariloche

Travel Guide 2025

A Traveler's Guide to Outdoor Adventures, Hidden Gems, and Local Culture in Bariloche, Argentina

Morgan Harper

4

Table of Contents

Chapter 1: Introduction to Bariloche

1.1 Overview of San Carlos de Bariloche

San Carlos de Bariloche, commonly referred to as Bariloche, is a picturesque city nestled in the Patagonia region of Argentina. Known for its stunning landscapes and outdoor activities, Bariloche is a favorite destination for travelers from around the world. Located in the province of Río Negro, the city sits on the southern shores of Lake Nahuel Huapi and is surrounded by the breathtaking Andes Mountains, making it a year-round hub for nature lovers, adventure seekers, and those simply in search of tranquility.

Bariloche is a place where visitors can experience the best of both worlds: it offers the charm of a small alpine town and the amenities of a modern, tourist-friendly city. With a population of around 130,000 people, it is the largest city in Argentina's Patagonian region. It serves as the capital of the Department of Los Lagos, which includes several other smaller towns and attractions.

The city's main draw is its natural beauty, with snow-capped mountains, crystal-clear lakes, dense forests, and abundant wildlife. The striking combination of these elements creates an ideal setting for outdoor activities such as skiing, hiking, fishing, and mountaineering. Moreover, its location in Patagonia gives visitors access to some of the most remote and unspoiled natural landscapes in the world, offering a haven for wildlife and a sense of isolation from the bustling cities of Argentina's more populated regions.

Bariloche also holds a significant place in Argentine tourism, serving as one of the most popular destinations in the country. The town's charming alpine-style architecture, combined with its picturesque surroundings, attracts visitors who come to explore both its outdoors and its cultural offerings. From the renowned chocolate shops to the local festivals and museums, Bariloche presents a unique fusion of nature and culture, making it a must-see destination for travelers.

1.2 Geography and Climate

Bariloche is located in the Argentine Patagonia, specifically in the Río Negro province. The city's geography is a combination of mountainous terrain, vast lakes, and dense forests. Bariloche lies on the southern edge of Lake Nahuel Huapi, one of the largest and most beautiful lakes in Argentina. The lake's crystal-clear waters stretch for over 500 square kilometers and are surrounded by the towering peaks of the Andes Mountains, including the iconic Mount Tronador to the west, a dormant volcano that rises over 3,400 meters above sea level.

The landscape around Bariloche is diverse, with dense forests of native trees, including coihue, lenga, and ñire, providing the perfect environment for wildlife such as deer, wild boar, and a variety of bird species. The area is also part of the Nahuel Huapi National Park, which covers more than 7,000 square kilometers and is one of Argentina's most important protected areas. The national park encompasses a variety of ecosystems, including forests, lakes, and high-altitude areas that are perfect for hiking, camping, and other outdoor activities.

The city itself is located at an altitude of approximately 800 meters above sea level, giving it a distinctive alpine atmosphere. Bariloche's geographic position near the Andes Mountains and the surrounding lakes plays a significant role in shaping its weather patterns. The region is subject to the effects of both oceanic and continental climates, which means it experiences significant variation in temperature and precipitation throughout the year.

Bariloche has a temperate climate with four distinct seasons: summer, fall, winter, and spring. Summers (from December to February) are generally mild, with temperatures ranging from 15°C to 25°C, though they can occasionally rise higher. This season is the most popular for outdoor activities such as hiking, fishing, and kayaking on the lakes. The fall months (March to May) bring cooler temperatures, with colorful autumn foliage providing a spectacular display of reds, yellows, and oranges. This is also a quieter time to visit, as the summer crowds start to thin out.

Winter (June to August) is the most famous season in Bariloche, as it transforms into a popular skiing and snowboarding destination. Temperatures often drop below freezing, and snowfall is frequent, especially in the higher altitudes of the surrounding mountains. The Cerro Catedral ski resort, located just outside the city, is one of South America's premier ski destinations, attracting winter sports enthusiasts from all over the world.

Spring (September to November) is a transitional period with cooler temperatures and a gradual warming trend. During this time, Bariloche's gardens and parks begin to bloom, creating a picturesque setting for outdoor activities. The season is also perfect for hiking and cycling as the weather becomes more favorable.

Due to its geographical location and climate, Bariloche offers a variety of activities throughout the year, catering to different interests depending on the season. Whether it's skiing in the winter, hiking in the summer, or enjoying the breathtaking views of the surrounding lakes and mountains during the fall and spring, Bariloche's geography makes it an all-season destination.

1.3 History and Cultural Heritage

The history of Bariloche is deeply intertwined with the indigenous peoples of Patagonia, the early explorers, and European settlers who shaped the region's development. Long before the arrival of Europeans, the area was inhabited by indigenous groups such as the Mapuche and the Puelche. These groups had a rich cultural heritage and lived off the land, hunting, fishing, and gathering resources from the forests, lakes, and mountains that surrounded them. The name "Bariloche" itself is derived from the Mapudungun word "Vuriloche," which means "people from behind the mountain," referring to the indigenous inhabitants who lived to the west of the Andes.

In the late 19th century, after Argentina's national borders were defined and the region was incorporated into the country,

Bariloche saw an influx of European settlers. Immigrants from Germany, Switzerland, and Austria began arriving in the area in the early 1900s, drawn by the region's natural beauty and the opportunity to establish agricultural and commercial ventures. These settlers brought with them their culture, architecture, and culinary traditions, which greatly influenced the development of Bariloche.

The city's architecture is a testament to the Swiss and German influence, with many buildings constructed in an alpine style that mirrors the design of towns in Europe's mountainous regions. This influence is especially visible in the numerous wooden houses, hotels, and the iconic Swiss-style architecture of the Civic Center, which remains one of Bariloche's main attractions today.

One of the most significant aspects of Bariloche's cultural heritage is its connection to chocolate. The city is renowned for its world-class chocolate shops, a legacy that traces back to the European settlers who introduced chocolate-making techniques to the region. Over the years, Bariloche has become known as the "chocolate capital" of Argentina, with dozens of artisanal chocolate shops dotting the streets of the city. The chocolate industry has grown to be an integral part of the local economy, and visitors can enjoy not only the delicious treats but also visit chocolate factories and learn about the history and craft of chocolate-making.

Bariloche's cultural heritage is also reflected in its arts and crafts, with local artisans producing handwoven textiles, ceramics, and woodwork that reflect the indigenous and European influences of the area. The city hosts a variety of cultural events and festivals throughout the year, showcasing local music, dance, and traditions that celebrate both the indigenous and European roots of the region. The Festival of Chocolate, held every year in July, is one such event that attracts thousands of visitors, offering a celebration of Bariloche's sweet heritage.

In addition to its European influences, Bariloche has a strong connection to the Argentine national identity. The city was officially founded on May 3, 1902, and over the decades, it has grown into an important hub for tourism, attracting visitors from across the globe. It was during the mid-20th century that Bariloche gained international fame as a tourist destination, with travelers flocking to its lakes and mountains for skiing, hiking, and other outdoor activities.

Today, Bariloche stands as a cultural melting pot, blending the traditions of its indigenous peoples with the European influence of its settlers, all while embracing its Argentine identity. This fusion of cultures makes Bariloche a unique destination, one that offers a rich history, breathtaking natural beauty, and a welcoming atmosphere for visitors from all walks of life.

Chapter 2: Getting to Bariloche

2.1 Major Airports and Transportation Options

San Carlos de Bariloche, affectionately known as Bariloche, is a prominent tourist destination in Argentina's Patagonia region. Its accessibility is facilitated through various transportation modes, ensuring visitors can reach this picturesque city with relative ease.

San Carlos de Bariloche International Airport (BRC)

The primary gateway to Bariloche is the San Carlos de Bariloche International Airport, officially named Teniente Luis Candelaria International Airport. Located approximately 13 kilometers east of the city center, the airport serves as a hub connecting Bariloche to major Argentine cities and select international destinations.

Facilities and Services:

- **Runways:** The airport boasts a single asphalt runway measuring 2,348 meters in length and 48 meters in width, accommodating various aircraft types.

- **Terminal:** The 12,000-square-meter terminal offers amenities such as duty-free shops, restaurants, currency exchange services, and free Wi-Fi, enhancing the travel experience for both domestic and international passengers.

Airlines and Destinations:

Several airlines operate regular flights to and from Bariloche Airport:

- **Domestic Flights:** Aerolíneas Argentinas, Flybondi, JetSMART, and LATAM Airlines offer flights connecting Bariloche to Buenos Aires, Córdoba, Mendoza, and other Argentine cities.

- **International Flights:** The airport provides direct flights to Santiago, Chile, and São Paulo, Brazil, with airlines such as LATAM and GOL Linhas Aéreas facilitating these routes.

Ground Transportation:

Upon arrival, visitors can choose from various ground transportation options:

- **Taxis and Remises:** Authorized taxi and remise (private car) services are available at the airport, offering direct transfers to hotels and other destinations in and around Bariloche.

- **Public Buses:** The local bus company, Mibus, operates routes connecting the airport to the city center, providing an economical option for travelers.

- **Car Rentals:** Several car rental agencies have counters at the airport, allowing travelers the flexibility to explore the region at their own pace.

2.2 Travel by Bus and Car

For those opting for overland travel, Bariloche is well-connected by an extensive network of roads and bus services.

By Bus:

Long-distance buses are a popular and affordable means of reaching Bariloche:

- **Bus Terminal:** The city's main bus terminal is centrally located, with services connecting Bariloche to Buenos Aires, Mendoza, Neuquén, and other Patagonian cities.

- **Bus Companies:** Numerous companies operate regular services, offering various comfort levels and amenities. It's advisable to book tickets in advance, especially during peak travel seasons.

By Car:

Renting a car provides flexibility and the opportunity to explore the scenic routes leading to Bariloche:

- **From Buenos Aires:** The drive from Buenos Aires to Bariloche covers approximately 1,600 kilometers, typically taking around 20 hours. The route passes through cities like Rosario and Córdoba, offering diverse landscapes.

- **From Mendoza:** Traveling from Mendoza involves a journey of about 1,100 kilometers, with an estimated driving time of 14 hours, passing through picturesque regions such as the Cuyo and Patagonia.

- **Road Conditions:** Major highways, such as Route 40 (Ruta Nacional 40) and Route 237 (Ruta Nacional 237), are paved and generally in good condition. However, it's essential to check current road conditions and travel advisories before embarking on the journey, especially during winter months when snow can affect certain routes.

2.3 Best Time to Visit

The optimal time to visit Bariloche largely depends on the activities you wish to pursue, as each season offers unique experiences.

Summer (December to February):

- **Weather:** Summer brings mild temperatures, with daytime highs averaging between 20°C to 30°C (68°F to 86°F). Nights can be cooler, so it's advisable to pack layers.

- **Activities:** This season is ideal for outdoor activities such as hiking, fishing, kayaking, and exploring the numerous national parks. The extended daylight hours provide ample time for exploration.

- **Festivals:** Summer also marks the time for local festivals and events, including music and cultural celebrations that showcase the region's heritage.

Autumn (March to May):

- **Weather:** Autumn brings cooler temperatures, with daytime highs ranging from 15°C to 22°C (59°F to 72°F). The season is characterized by crisp air and colorful foliage.

- **Activities:** It's an excellent time for photography, hiking, and enjoying the tranquil beauty of the region as the summer crowds diminish.

- **Events:** The autumn months may feature local harvest festivals and cultural events that highlight the region's traditions and gastronomy.

Winter (June to August):

- **Weather:** Winter transforms Bariloche into a snowy wonderland, with temperatures often dropping below freezing. Snowfall is common, especially in the surrounding mountains.

- **Activities:** This is the prime season for winter sports enthusiasts. The Cerro Catedral ski resort offers world-class skiing and snowboarding facilities.

- **Festivals:** Winter also brings events such as the National Snow Festival, celebrating the season's unique offerings with snow sculptures, music, and cultural activities.

Spring (September to November):

- **Weather:** Spring sees a gradual warming, with daytime temperatures ranging from 10°C to 18°C (50°F to 64°F). The landscape begins to bloom, offering vibrant colors.

- **Activities:** It's a favorable time for hiking, birdwatching, and enjoying the rejuvenated natural surroundings. The trails are less crowded, providing a peaceful experience.

- **Events:** Spring may host environmental awareness programs and outdoor concerts that celebrate the season's arrival.

Considerations:

- **Peak Seasons:** Summer and winter are peak tourist seasons in Bariloche. If you prefer to avoid crowds and higher prices, consider visiting during the shoulder seasons of autumn or spring.

- **Accommodation:** Regardless of the season, it's advisable to book accommodations and activities in advance, especially during holidays and local festivals, to ensure availability.

- **Weather Preparedness:** Weather in Bariloche can be unpredictable. It's recommended to check forecasts regularly and pack accordingly, including waterproof clothing and sun protection.

Chapter 3: Accommodation in Bariloche

Bariloche, nestled in Argentina's Patagonia region, offers a diverse array of accommodations to suit various preferences and budgets. From luxurious lakeside resorts to cozy hostels, the city caters to travelers seeking comfort, adventure, and unique experiences.

3.1 Luxury Hotels

For travelers seeking unparalleled comfort and world-class amenities, Bariloche boasts several luxury establishments that provide exceptional experiences:

Llao Llao Hotel & Resort

Situated within the Nahuel Huapi National Park, Llao Llao Hotel & Resort is an iconic luxury destination. The resort offers panoramic views of the surrounding lakes and mountains, combining elegant architecture with natural beauty. Guests can enjoy amenities such as a championship golf course, a full-service spa, and fine dining options.

Charming Luxury Lodge & Private Spa

Located on the shores of Lake Moreno, this boutique hotel offers a serene retreat with personalized service. Each suite features a private spa, complete with a hot tub and sauna, ensuring a relaxing stay. The property also boasts an indoor pool, a wine cellar, and a restaurant serving Patagonian cuisine.

El Casco Art Hotel

Combining luxury with art, El Casco Art Hotel is situated on the shores of Lake Nahuel Huapi. The hotel features a vast collection of Argentine art, offering guests a cultural experience alongside modern amenities. Facilities include an indoor pool, a spa, and a restaurant with panoramic lake views.

3.2 Mid-Range Hotels

For travelers seeking comfort without extravagance, Bariloche offers a selection of mid-range accommodations that provide quality services and amenities:

Arelauquen Lodge, A Tribute Portfolio Hotel

Nestled within the Arelauquen Golf & Country Club, this lodge offers spacious rooms with views of the golf course or surrounding mountains. Guests can enjoy amenities such as an outdoor pool, a spa, and proximity to outdoor activities like hiking and fishing.

Hotel Tres Reyes

Located in the city center, Hotel Tres Reyes offers comfortable rooms with modern decor. The hotel features an indoor pool, a fitness center, and a restaurant serving regional cuisine. Its central location provides easy access to local shops and attractions.

Hotel Panamericano Bariloche

Offering panoramic views of Lake Nahuel Huapi, Hotel Panamericano provides comfortable rooms with contemporary design. Amenities include a heated outdoor pool, a fitness center, and a restaurant specializing in Patagonian cuisine.

3.3 Budget-Friendly Lodging

Bariloche caters to budget-conscious travelers with a variety of affordable lodging options that do not compromise on comfort:

Bella Vista Refugio Urbano

A cozy hostel located near the city center, Bella Vista offers both private rooms and dormitories. Guests can enjoy a communal kitchen, a lounge area, and organized activities, making it a great choice for social travelers.

Alpino Hostel Boutique Bariloche

Situated within walking distance of the Civic Centre, this boutique hostel offers private and shared accommodations.

Guests can enjoy a communal kitchen, a garden, and a terrace with panoramic city views.

La Costa del Pueblo Hostel

Located in the heart of Bariloche, this hostel provides dormitory-style rooms and private rooms at affordable rates. Facilities include a communal kitchen, a bar, and a lounge area, creating a friendly and relaxed atmosphere.

3.4 Unique Stays (Cabins, Lodges, and Hostels)

For travelers seeking distinctive lodging experiences, Bariloche offers unique accommodations that blend comfort with the region's natural beauty:

Isla Victoria Lodge

Accessible only by boat, Isla Victoria Lodge offers an exclusive retreat on a private island in Lake Nahuel Huapi. The lodge features rustic-chic rooms, gourmet dining, and a range of outdoor activities, including hiking and fishing.

Rio Manso Lodge

Located near the border with Chile, Rio Manso Lodge offers a secluded experience surrounded by Patagonian wilderness. The lodge provides comfortable rooms, a restaurant serving local cuisine, and guided excursions to explore the pristine environment.

Alberto's Old Cabin

For a truly unique experience, consider staying in Alberto's Old Cabin, a restored cabin offering a rustic and authentic Patagonian experience. Located in a secluded area, guests can enjoy tranquility and proximity to nature, with opportunities for hiking and wildlife observation

Tips for Choosing Accommodation in Bariloche

- **Seasonal Considerations:** Bariloche experiences peak tourist seasons during the summer (December to February) and winter (June to August). It's advisable to book accommodations well in advance during these periods to secure preferred lodging.

- **Location:** Consider the proximity of your accommodation to the activities you plan to engage in. Lodging near the ski resorts is ideal for winter sports enthusiasts, while lakeside accommodations are perfect for summer water activities.

- **Amenities:** Determine the amenities that are important to you, such as free Wi-Fi, breakfast options, or pet-friendly policies, to ensure a comfortable stay.

- **Local Experience:** For a more immersive experience, consider accommodations that offer cultural insights, such as lodges featuring local art or hostels that organize community events.

Bariloche's diverse accommodation landscape ensures that every traveler can find a suitable place to stay, whether seeking luxury, affordability, or a unique lodging experience amidst the stunning Patagonian scenery.

Chapter 4: Top Attractions and Landmarks

Bariloche, nestled in Argentina's Patagonia region, is renowned for its breathtaking natural beauty and rich cultural heritage. The city and its surroundings offer a plethora of attractions that cater to a wide range of interests. From pristine lakes and majestic mountains to historical sites and cultural institutions, Bariloche promises memorable experiences for every traveler.

4.1 Nahuel Huapi Lake

Nahuel Huapi Lake is the largest in Argentina's Lake District, covering approximately 557 square kilometers. The lake is renowned for its crystal-clear waters, surrounded by snow-capped mountains and lush forests, offering a picturesque setting for various activities.

Activities and Attractions:

- **Boat Tours:** Visitors can embark on boat excursions to explore the lake's numerous islands and secluded beaches, providing unique perspectives of the surrounding landscapes.

- **Fishing:** The lake is abundant with trout and salmon, making it a popular destination for anglers seeking both relaxation and sport.

- **Beaches:** During the summer months, beaches such as Playa Bonita become lively spots for sunbathing, swimming, and picnicking, offering facilities and amenities for families and groups.

- **Hiking:** Trails along the shoreline and into the adjacent forests cater to various skill levels, allowing hikers to immerse themselves in the region's natural beauty.

4.2 Cerro Catedral Ski Resort

Cerro Catedral, also known as Cerro Catedral Alta Patagonia, is South America's largest ski resort, attracting winter sports enthusiasts from around the globe. Located approximately 25 kilometers southwest of Bariloche, the resort offers diverse terrains suitable for all levels of skiers and snowboarders.

Features and Activities:

- **Skiing and Snowboarding:** With numerous slopes and modern lift systems, the resort provides extensive opportunities for winter sports, complemented by stunning panoramic views.

- **Snowshoeing and Snowboarding:** For those seeking alternative snow activities, the resort offers marked trails and equipment rentals, ensuring a unique experience amidst the snowy landscapes.

- **Mountain Dining:** Several mountain huts and restaurants offer warm meals and beverages, allowing visitors to rest and enjoy the alpine ambiance.

- **Summer Activities:** During the warmer months, the resort transforms into a hub for mountain biking, hiking, and paragliding, catering to adventure seekers year-round.

4.3 Cerro Otto and the Cable Car

Cerro Otto stands at 1,405 meters and offers some of the most panoramic views of Bariloche and its surroundings. Accessible via a modern cable car, the summit provides a 360-degree perspective of the city, lakes, and mountains.

Highlights:

- **Panoramic Views:** The observation deck at the summit allows visitors to capture breathtaking photographs and fully appreciate the region's natural beauty.

- **Dining Experience:** At the top, a revolving restaurant offers a unique dining experience, where guests can enjoy local cuisine while slowly rotating to take in the expansive views.

- **Recreational Activities:** The area around the summit features hiking and mountain biking trails, suitable for various skill levels, encouraging visitors to engage with the natural environment actively.

4.4 Isla Victoria and Arrayanes Forest

Isla Victoria is the largest island in Nahuel Huapi Lake, known for its diverse ecosystems and rich biodiversity. Adjacent to the island is the Arrayanes Forest, famed for its unique arrayán trees with distinctive cinnamon-colored bark.

Experiences:

- **Guided Tours:** Boat tours from Bariloche provide guided visits to Isla Victoria, where trails wind through dense forests, offering opportunities to observe native flora and fauna.

- **Arrayanes Forest:** A highlight of the island, the Arrayanes Forest features a loop trail that winds through ancient trees, some over 600 years old, providing a surreal and enchanting experience.

- **Camping and Picnicking:** Designated areas on Isla Victoria allow visitors to camp under the stars or enjoy picnics amidst the tranquil surroundings, fostering a deep connection with nature.

4.5 The Civic Center and Museo de la Patagonia

The Civic Center of Bariloche is a central hub that combines historical architecture with cultural institutions, reflecting the city's heritage and community spirit. Adjacent to the Civic Center is the Museo de la Patagonia, offering insights into the region's natural and cultural history.

Features:

- **Civic Center Architecture:** Constructed in the early 20th century, the Civic Center showcases alpine-style architecture with its wooden structures and stone buildings, creating a warm and inviting atmosphere.

- **Museo de la Patagonia:** Housed within the Civic Center, the museum features exhibits on the region's indigenous cultures, geological formations, flora, and fauna, providing a comprehensive understanding of

Patagonia's rich history.

- **Cultural Events:** The Civic Center area frequently hosts cultural events, including art exhibitions, music performances, and local markets, fostering community engagement and offering visitors a taste of local life.

Bariloche's top attractions and landmarks offer a harmonious blend of natural wonders and cultural treasures, ensuring that every visitor finds something to marvel at. Whether it's exploring the serene waters of Nahuel Huapi Lake, conquering the slopes of Cerro Catedral, ascending the heights of Cerro Otto, wandering through the enchanting forests of Isla Victoria, or immersing oneself in the local culture at the Civic Center and Museo de la Patagonia, Bariloche promises experiences that are both enriching and unforgettable.

Chapter 5: Outdoor Adventures

Bariloche, located in Argentina's Patagonia region, is not just a picturesque destination but also an adventurer's paradise. With its awe-inspiring mountains, lush forests, clear lakes, and vast wilderness, it offers an array of outdoor activities for nature lovers and thrill-seekers. Whether you're looking for peaceful hikes, winter sports, or water adventures, Bariloche caters to all kinds of explorers. This chapter delves into the top outdoor adventures you can enjoy in Bariloche.

5.1 Hiking and Trekking Trails

Bariloche is a mecca for hiking and trekking enthusiasts. Surrounded by the stunning landscapes of the Andes and Nahuel Huapi National Park, it offers trails that cater to all levels of hikers. Whether you're a beginner looking for a scenic walk or an experienced trekker seeking a challenging multi-day hike, Bariloche has something for you.

Popular Hiking Trails:

- **Cerro Campanario**

  One of the most popular short hikes in Bariloche is the Cerro Campanario trail. The summit offers panoramic views of the city, lakes, and surrounding mountains. The hike takes about 45 minutes to an hour and is of moderate difficulty. Alternatively, visitors can take a chairlift to the top and enjoy the same magnificent views with minimal effort.

- **Refugio Frey**

  The hike to Refugio Frey, located in the Catedral Mountain range, is a challenging 7-hour round-trip journey. This trek is popular among experienced hikers due to its steep paths and rugged terrain. However, the reward at the end is well worth it: a stunning alpine landscape with lakes and towering peaks. Refugio Frey serves as a resting point, providing food, shelter, and warmth to trekkers.

- **Cerro Tronador**

  For those seeking a more strenuous adventure, the Cerro Tronador hike is a must. This trail takes trekkers up one of the highest peaks in the region, standing at 3,400 meters. The trek takes multiple days, with trekkers camping along the way. The highlight of this hike is the chance to see glaciers up close and the impressive "Black

Glacier," which is one of the main draws.

- **Laguna Negra**

  Laguna Negra offers a picturesque trek that leads to a stunning glacial lake surrounded by rugged mountains. The hike to Laguna Negra takes around 6-7 hours, and it's a moderately difficult trail. Along the way, hikers will pass through forests, alpine meadows, and rocky landscapes.

- **Los Alerces National Park**

  Located a short drive from Bariloche, Los Alerces National Park is home to an array of stunning trails. The park is famous for its ancient forests of alerce trees, some of which are over 3,000 years old. Trails range from short walks to longer treks, all offering beautiful views of lakes, forests, and wildlife.

Why Hike in Bariloche?

Bariloche's natural beauty offers an ever-changing landscape, making every hike a memorable experience. Whether it's the towering peaks, tranquil lakes, dense forests, or wildlife sightings, hiking in Bariloche provides an escape into nature and an opportunity to explore one of Argentina's most pristine wilderness areas.

5.2 Skiing and Snowboarding in the Winter

Bariloche's snow-capped mountains make it a premier winter sports destination in South America. From June to October, the region becomes a paradise for skiers and snowboarders, thanks to Cerro Catedral, one of the largest ski resorts in South America.

Cerro Catedral Ski Resort

- **Overview of Cerro Catedral**
  Cerro Catedral (also known as Catedral Alta Patagonia) is the crown jewel of Argentina's ski resorts. It boasts a vast skiable area of 1,200 hectares, with 120 km of slopes suited for all levels of skiers and snowboarders. The resort features modern ski lifts, snowboarding parks, and excellent facilities, making it one of the most popular winter destinations in the Southern Hemisphere.

- **Skiing and Snowboarding**
  Cerro Catedral's slopes offer something for everyone. Beginners can take lessons at the ski school and enjoy the easier slopes near the base. Intermediate and advanced skiers will love the wide variety of runs, from forested trails to thrilling downhill descents. The resort is also home to multiple terrain parks for snowboarders looking for some extra excitement. Snowboarders can enjoy ramps, jumps, and rails to perfect their skills.

- **Snow Conditions**

  The snow conditions at Cerro Catedral are typically excellent during the peak winter months of July and August. The resort's location at the base of the Andes ensures consistent snowfall, and it is equipped with snowmaking machines that guarantee good conditions even when natural snowfall is light.

- **Other Activities**

  Aside from skiing and snowboarding, visitors can also enjoy other winter activities such as snowshoeing, snowmobiling, and tobogganing. For those looking to relax, there are plenty of cozy cafés and restaurants where you can enjoy traditional Argentine cuisine, including hot chocolate, fondue, and grilled meats.

Why Ski or Snowboard in Bariloche?

Cerro Catedral offers a world-class ski experience with breathtaking views of Lake Nahuel Huapi, the surrounding mountains, and pristine forests. With a range of activities both on and off the slopes, it's an ideal location for both beginners and seasoned winter sports enthusiasts.

5.3 Water Sports: Kayaking, Fishing, and Sailing

Bariloche's lakes, particularly Nahuel Huapi, are perfect for water-based activities. Surrounded by towering peaks and dense forests, the crystal-clear waters offer a stunning backdrop for a variety of water sports.

Kayaking and Canoeing

- **Lakes and Rivers**
  Bariloche is a great location for kayaking, whether you're looking to explore the serene shores of Nahuel Huapi Lake or navigate the fast-moving rivers of Patagonia. Guided kayaking tours offer opportunities to explore hidden coves, remote beaches, and scenic landscapes that can only be accessed by boat.

- **Laguna El Trébol**
  Another popular spot for kayaking is Laguna El Trébol, a smaller lake near Bariloche. Its calm waters make it perfect for beginners or those who want a relaxing paddle through nature.

Fishing

- **Fly Fishing**
  Fishing enthusiasts flock to Bariloche to experience some

of the best fly fishing in Argentina. Nahuel Huapi Lake and the nearby rivers offer excellent fishing opportunities, particularly for rainbow trout, brown trout, and brook trout. The region's remote lakes and rivers provide pristine, unspoiled conditions, making it a great destination for both beginners and experienced anglers.

- **Guided Fishing Tours**
  There are several professional guides available who can take you to the best fishing spots. These guides know the local waters inside out and provide everything you need for a successful day of fishing.

Sailing

- **Sailing on Nahuel Huapi Lake**
  Sailing is another fantastic way to explore the waters of Nahuel Huapi Lake. Whether you are an experienced sailor or a beginner, there are options for you. Several companies in Bariloche offer boat rentals and guided sailing tours, allowing you to enjoy the stunning views while navigating the tranquil waters.

- **Charter Services**
  For a more luxurious experience, visitors can charter private boats for a personalized sailing tour. You can spend the day cruising around the lake, stopping at secluded beaches or islands for a picnic.

Why Water Sports in Bariloche?

With its clear, blue lakes and mountainous surroundings, Bariloche offers some of the most scenic water sports destinations in the world. Whether you're paddling through peaceful waters, casting a line in search of the perfect catch, or gliding across the lake on a sailboat, Bariloche provides an unforgettable experience for water sports enthusiasts.

5.4 Mountain Biking and Scenic Drives

Bariloche's diverse terrain makes it an excellent destination for mountain biking. The combination of dirt trails, forest paths, and mountain tracks offers cyclists an adrenaline-packed experience, while the region's scenic drives provide a more leisurely way to take in the breathtaking views.

Mountain Biking

- **Circuito Chico**
  The Circuito Chico is a popular biking route that circles the outskirts of Bariloche, offering incredible views of lakes, mountains, and forests. This relatively easy route is around 27 kilometers long, making it suitable for most cyclists. Along the way, cyclists can stop at scenic viewpoints, beaches, and forests, and enjoy the peaceful atmosphere.

- **Cerro Otto Trails**
  For more experienced bikers, the trails around Cerro Otto offer a more challenging experience. The ascent can be steep, and the terrain is rugged, but the reward is a thrilling ride with spectacular views.

- **Lake Moreno and Beyond**
  For advanced riders, the roads around Lake Moreno and beyond offer more difficult and technical trails. These routes take you through dense forests and rugged terrain, providing an adventurous cycling experience with sweeping views of the mountains and lakes.

Scenic Drives

- **Route 40**
  The iconic Route 40 runs through Bariloche, connecting the city with the rest of Patagonia. This scenic drive offers travelers the chance to experience the diverse landscapes of the region, from lush forests to arid plains and towering mountain peaks. Route 40 is also a key route to explore other parts of Argentina's Lake District.

- **The Road to Refugio Frey**
  This scenic drive takes visitors up to the trailhead for the Refugio Frey hike. Along the way, you'll pass through beautiful valleys and forests, offering an excellent

opportunity to enjoy the stunning views of the surrounding mountains.

Why Mountain Biking and Scenic Drives in Bariloche?

Bariloche's rugged landscapes provide the perfect setting for cyclists and road-trip enthusiasts. Whether you're tackling mountain trails or simply enjoying a leisurely drive, Bariloche offers endless opportunities to explore its natural beauty at your own pace.

5.5 Scenic Tours: Circuito Chico and More

Bariloche is famous for its scenic tours, which allow visitors to experience the region's natural beauty in a more relaxed way.

Circuito Chico

- **Overview of Circuito Chico**
  The Circuito Chico is a 60-kilometer loop that takes visitors through some of the most picturesque areas surrounding Bariloche. This scenic drive includes stops at several important landmarks, such as Cerro Campanario, Playa Bonita, and the historic Llao Llao Hotel. It's a popular option for tourists who want to experience the beauty of the region without engaging in strenuous activities.

- **Guided Tours**

  Many companies offer guided tours of the Circuito Chico, providing detailed information about the history and geology of the area. These tours often include stops for photography, nature walks, and a meal at one of the local eateries.

Why Scenic Tours in Bariloche?

For those who prefer a more relaxed experience, the scenic tours in Bariloche offer a comprehensive overview of the area's natural beauty. Whether you're driving or joining a guided tour, the views are simply unforgettable, making it a must-do for any visitor.

Bariloche is a true paradise for outdoor adventurers, offering everything from hiking and skiing to water sports and scenic drives. Whether you're a thrill-seeker looking for a challenge or someone simply wanting to explore the stunning beauty of Patagonia, Bariloche promises an unforgettable experience.

Chapter 6: Bariloche's Unique Cuisine

Bariloche, located in Argentina's Patagonia region, is not only famous for its breathtaking landscapes and outdoor adventures but also for its rich and diverse culinary scene. Influenced by Argentina's history, geography, and the European immigrants who settled in the area, Bariloche offers a unique blend of flavors, with local dishes that highlight the best of Patagonian and Argentine cuisine. In this chapter, we will explore the traditional Argentine dishes you must try, the impact of Swiss and German cuisines, the city's renowned chocolate shops, and the best restaurants and cafes in Bariloche.

6.1 Traditional Argentine Dishes to Try

Argentine cuisine is well-known for its hearty, flavorful dishes that are influenced by the country's agricultural practices, its climate, and its rich cultural history. In Bariloche, the region's cuisine draws inspiration from the Patagonian landscape, known for its rich meats, fresh fish, and unique vegetables. Here are some of the traditional Argentine dishes you should try while in Bariloche.

Asado (Argentine Barbecue)

No visit to Argentina is complete without trying asado, the Argentine version of barbecue. Asado is not just a meal but a cultural event, and in Bariloche, it takes on a special significance. The Patagonian region is famous for its high-quality beef, which is raised on vast plains and grazing fields. The most traditional cuts for asado include bife de chorizo (sirloin), entraña (skirt steak), and costillas (ribs). In Bariloche, asado is often enjoyed with a chimichurri sauce, which is made of parsley, garlic, vinegar, and olive oil.

Asado is usually cooked over an open flame or on a grill (called a parrilla). The slow-cooked meat is often served with traditional sides such as papas fritas (fried potatoes), ensalada rusa (a salad made of potatoes, carrots, and peas), and provoleta, a grilled provolone cheese that's a true Argentine delight. In Bariloche, you'll find many local parrillas (steakhouses) that serve delicious asado alongside a selection of regional wines.

Cordero Patagónico (Patagonian Lamb)

Patagonia is known for its tender, flavorful lamb, and cordero is one of the most iconic dishes of the region. The lamb is typically roasted on a spit (known as cordero al asador), and the meat is cooked slowly over an open flame, giving it a smoky, rich flavor. In Bariloche, you'll find this dish served with papas a la crema (creamy potatoes) or ensaladas (salads) that include local ingredients like red cabbage and lettuce.

The method of roasting the lamb on a spit is a tradition that has been passed down through generations, making it an essential part of Bariloche's culinary heritage. The combination of tender lamb and the earthy flavors of Patagonia's herbs and wood-fired cooking makes cordero patagónico a must-try for any visitor.

Empanadas

Another traditional Argentine dish to try in Bariloche is empanadas, which are pastry pockets filled with a variety of fillings such as minced meat, cheese, onions, and spinach. Empanadas are a popular snack or appetizer in Argentina, and Bariloche offers some unique twists on the dish. In the Patagonian region, empanadas de cordero (lamb empanadas) are a favorite, where the rich lamb filling is seasoned with local spices and herbs.

Empanadas are typically baked or fried, and they can be found at restaurants, cafes, and street food vendors throughout Bariloche. Whether enjoyed as a quick snack or as part of a larger meal, empanadas are a delicious reflection of Argentina's culinary traditions.

Trucha (Trout)

The lakes surrounding Bariloche are home to many species of fish, including the famous trucha (trout), which is a local delicacy. The clear, cold waters of Lake Nahuel Huapi provide ideal conditions for trout to thrive, and the fish is often served grilled, baked, or fried. It's typically accompanied by papas al natural (boiled potatoes), verduras (vegetables), or a simple ensalada (salad).

Trout in Bariloche is especially known for its fresh, delicate flavor. Many restaurants in the city feature trucha on their menus, with variations that include roasted garlic, lemon, and fresh herbs.

6.2 The Influence of Swiss and German Cuisine

Bariloche has a long history of European immigration, particularly from Switzerland and Germany, which has heavily influenced the local cuisine. Swiss and German immigrants brought with them their culinary traditions, and over time, these have been adapted to fit the region's local ingredients and tastes.

Swiss-Inspired Dishes

Swiss immigrants to Bariloche were particularly influential in shaping the city's dairy culture, and one of the most notable culinary contributions is cheese. The alpine climate of Bariloche closely resembles that of Switzerland, which helped foster the production of high-quality cheese. Traditional Swiss cheeses like Gruyère, Emmental, and Raclette are popular in Bariloche and are used in a variety of dishes.

One of the most beloved Swiss-inspired dishes in Bariloche is fondue. Fondue, typically made from melted cheese, is perfect for the cold Patagonian winters. It is often served with bread, vegetables, and potatoes for dipping, creating a warm, communal dining experience that is beloved by locals and tourists alike.

German-Inspired Dishes

German immigrants also left their mark on Bariloche's culinary landscape, particularly with the introduction of sausages and hearty stews. Käsespätzle, a German noodle dish made with cheese and caramelized onions, is a favorite among locals and can often be found on restaurant menus in Bariloche.

Another German influence is sauerbraten, a slow-braised beef dish marinated in vinegar and spices. The German-style sausages, particularly bratwurst, are also commonly served in Bariloche, often paired with mustard, sauerkraut, and kartoffelsalat (potato salad). These German-inspired dishes are often enjoyed in Bariloche's traditional cervecerías (beer halls) and restaurants, offering a hearty and satisfying meal.

Influence on Pastries

Swiss and German immigrants also contributed to Bariloche's reputation as a haven for baked goods. Traditional pastries like strudel, apfelstrudel (apple strudel), and kuchen (cakes) are often served in local cafes. The delicate pastries, filled with fruits, nuts, or custard, are often paired with coffee and enjoyed as a sweet treat.

6.3 Chocolate Shops: A Sweet Experience

One of the most delightful aspects of Bariloche's cuisine is its world-renowned chocolate. Bariloche has earned the nickname "Argentina's chocolate capital" due to the large number of artisanal chocolate shops that line its streets. The city's chocolate-making tradition began in the early 20th century when European immigrants, particularly from Switzerland and Germany, brought their chocolate-making techniques to the region. Today, Bariloche is home to some of the best chocolate in the world.

Local Chocolate Shops

Bariloche boasts dozens of chocolate shops, each offering a wide variety of chocolate products made with the finest ingredients. From handmade truffles to chocolate bars, pralines, and hot chocolate, there's something for every chocolate lover. Some of the most famous chocolate shops in Bariloche include:

- **Rapa Nui**
  This family-owned shop is one of the most popular in Bariloche. Known for its rich, high-quality chocolates, Rapa Nui offers a range of products, from artisanal truffles to beautifully crafted chocolate figures.

- **Mamuschka**
  Another famous chocolate shop in Bariloche,

Mamuschka is known for its decadent chocolate truffles and pralines. Their store offers a cozy atmosphere where you can sit down and enjoy a warm cup of chocolate or purchase chocolates as souvenirs.

- **Del Turista**
  Del Turista is one of the oldest chocolate shops in Bariloche, offering a wide selection of handcrafted chocolates. Their rich, smooth truffles are particularly popular among visitors.

Chocolate Tours

For those looking to learn more about Bariloche's chocolate-making history, there are guided tours available. These tours typically include visits to local chocolate factories, where visitors can watch the chocolate-making process and sample various types of chocolate. Some tours even allow guests to try their hand at making their own chocolates.

6.4 Best Restaurants and Cafes in Bariloche

Bariloche's culinary scene is diverse, with a mix of traditional Argentine dishes, European influences, and modern gastronomy. Whether you're in the mood for a casual meal, a fine dining experience, or a cozy cafe to enjoy some local pastries, Bariloche has something to offer.

Fine Dining

- **El Boliche de Alberto**

  For an authentic Argentine dining experience, El Boliche de Alberto is a must-visit. Known for its asado and Patagonian specialties, this restaurant offers a warm, inviting atmosphere. The lamb and steak are among the best in Bariloche, and their extensive wine list showcases Argentina's best wines.

- **La Costa del Pueblo**

  This fine-dining establishment offers a combination of Argentine and Patagonian cuisine with a modern twist. The menu includes a variety of grilled meats, seafood, and pasta dishes, and the restaurant is known for its stylish decor and excellent service.

Cafes and Casual Dining

- **Café de la Plaza**

  Located in the heart of Bariloche's Civic Center, Café de la Plaza is a cozy spot where visitors can enjoy a hot cup of coffee and a selection of pastries. It's a great place to relax and people-watch, while savoring traditional Argentine cakes such as chocotorta (chocolate biscuit cake) or tarta de manzana (apple pie).

- **La Plaza**

  La Plaza is a casual cafe that serves delicious sandwiches, pastries, and coffee. It's a popular spot among locals for breakfast or a mid-afternoon snack. The café also offers a selection of locally made chocolates and ice creams, making it a perfect place to indulge your sweet tooth.

Casual Dining and Street Food

- **El Patio de la Plaza**

  El Patio de la Plaza is a great place for casual dining, offering a selection of Argentine street food favorites like empanadas, choripán (sausage sandwich), and milanesa (breaded meat cutlet). The restaurant has a relaxed vibe and is ideal for a quick bite after a day of sightseeing.

- **La Bella Roma**

  For pizza lovers, La Bella Roma offers a variety of delicious pizzas with fresh ingredients. This family-friendly restaurant is known for its cozy atmosphere and large portions.

Bariloche's cuisine is a true reflection of its unique location at the crossroads of Argentine, Swiss, and German influences. From the traditional asado and cordero patagónico to the indulgence of artisanal chocolates and the hearty, comforting dishes brought by European immigrants, Bariloche offers a culinary journey as diverse and captivating as its landscapes.

Chapter 7: Shopping in Bariloche

Bariloche, with its blend of breathtaking landscapes and rich cultural heritage, offers a shopping experience that reflects both its natural beauty and its diverse history. From unique handcrafted goods made by local artisans to the world-renowned chocolate and wines that the region produces, shopping in Bariloche allows visitors to take home a piece of Patagonia. Whether you're looking for a one-of-a-kind souvenir or indulging in some of Argentina's finest offerings, Bariloche's shopping scene is as varied and fascinating as its landscapes. This chapter explores the different shopping experiences available in Bariloche, including handcrafted goods, souvenirs, markets, and shopping centers.

7.1 Handcrafted Goods and Local Artisans

Bariloche is home to a wide array of local artisans who create beautiful handmade goods that reflect the cultural traditions and natural resources of Patagonia. These artisanal products are not only unique but also deeply rooted in the region's history and environment. Shopping for these handcrafted items provides a meaningful connection to the area and supports local craftspeople.

Woodwork and Leather Goods

One of the most famous types of handcrafted goods in Bariloche is its woodwork. The city is situated in a forested area, and many local artisans use the abundant wood from the surrounding forests to create intricate wooden products. You'll find a variety of hand-carved items, including furniture, small decorative pieces, and kitchenware. Popular items include wooden bowls, cutting boards, and picture frames, which showcase the skill and artistry of the local woodworkers.

Leather goods are another significant part of the local artisan scene. Many shops in Bariloche sell finely crafted leather products such as jackets, wallets, belts, and boots. These products are made using high-quality leather, often sourced from local tanneries, and are designed to be both durable and stylish, blending traditional techniques with modern designs.

Woven Textiles

The Andean region, including Bariloche, has a long tradition of weaving, which is reflected in the many handcrafted textiles available in the city. Local artisans weave scarves, shawls, blankets, and ponchos, often using natural dyes and fibers. These textiles are made with alpaca, sheep wool, and sometimes even llama wool, providing both warmth and luxury. Visitors will find vibrant, hand-woven patterns that reflect the colors and textures of Patagonia's natural environment.

The most popular textiles in Bariloche are the colorful ponchos and rebozos (woven shawls), which are perfect souvenirs for anyone seeking warmth and authenticity. These pieces are ideal for those wanting to experience the craftsmanship of Patagonia's indigenous and local cultures.

Silver Jewelry

Another popular handcrafted item in Bariloche is silver jewelry. The region has a long history of silversmithing, and many local artisans create stunning jewelry inspired by Patagonia's landscape and indigenous culture. Silver jewelry featuring stones like turquoise, amethyst, and garnet is particularly sought after, as these designs evoke the colors and natural beauty of the surrounding mountains and lakes.

Shops specializing in silver jewelry often feature rings, bracelets, necklaces, and earrings that are both delicate and bold, making them a great gift or personal keepsake. The designs range from minimalist, geometric shapes to more intricate pieces that incorporate local symbols and motifs.

Where to Find Handcrafted Goods

Bariloche is home to numerous artisan shops and markets that sell these handmade goods. The **Civic Center** area, particularly along the main streets such as **Mitre Street**, is dotted with small boutique shops and galleries where visitors can browse and purchase high-quality handcrafted products. Many of these stores are owned by local artisans, allowing shoppers to meet the creators of their purchases and learn about their techniques.

In addition to the shops, there are also annual artisan fairs in Bariloche, where local artists gather to display their work. These fairs often take place during the summer months, providing an excellent opportunity to meet artisans and purchase unique, one-of-a-kind items.

7.2 Shopping for Souvenirs: Chocolates, Wines, and Crafts

When it comes to souvenirs, Bariloche offers some of the best products that reflect the region's unique flavors, traditions, and craftsmanship. Chocolates, wines, and crafts are among the most popular items for visitors looking to take a piece of Patagonia home with them.

Chocolates

As the chocolate capital of Argentina, Bariloche is famous for its high-quality artisanal chocolates. The city's history of chocolate-making began with Swiss and German immigrants who brought their traditional recipes and techniques to the region. Today, Bariloche is home to a wide range of chocolate shops offering everything from classic chocolate bars to decadent pralines and truffles.

Some of the most well-known chocolate brands in Bariloche include Rapa Nui, Mamuschka, and Del Turista. These shops offer a wide variety of handcrafted chocolates, including rich dark chocolate, milk chocolate, and chocolate with unique fillings such as dulce de leche, fruit, and nuts. Many shops also offer chocolate spreads and hot chocolate mixes, perfect for gifting or enjoying at home.

For those interested in learning about the chocolate-making process, some of Bariloche's chocolate shops offer guided tours where visitors can observe chocolatiers at work and sample different types of chocolate. Buying chocolates from Bariloche is a must-do for anyone with a sweet tooth, and it makes for an excellent and indulgent souvenir.

Patagonian Wines

Argentina is renowned for its wines, and Bariloche is no exception. The region around Bariloche is known for its unique microclimates, which produce high-quality wines, particularly Pinot Noir, Merlot, and Malbec. Many wine shops in the city offer a selection of Patagonian wines, including bottles from local vineyards in the Neuquén and Río Negro provinces.

If you're looking for a gift or souvenir that showcases Argentina's world-class wine culture, consider purchasing a bottle of Patagonian wine. Many shops and wine boutiques in Bariloche offer wines directly from the region's best vineyards, and you can often find wine tasting sessions to sample the best offerings.

Local Crafts and Souvenirs

In addition to handcrafted goods like textiles and woodwork, Bariloche also offers a wide range of other local crafts. Many shops sell souvenirs such as maté gourds and bombillas (metal straws used for drinking maté, a traditional Argentine tea), calabazas (hand-painted gourds), and leather-bound journals. These items make great gifts or mementos of your trip to Patagonia.

Another popular souvenir is ceramics, particularly hand-painted pottery and decorative items. Local artists create beautiful bowls, plates, and decorative figurines that showcase the colors and themes of the region. These items often feature indigenous patterns and motifs, making them both culturally significant and visually striking.

Where to Buy Souvenirs

Bariloche has several shops and local markets where you can find these delicious treats and crafts. Many of the best chocolate shops, wineries, and craft stores are concentrated around the Civic Center and Mitre Street, which is lined with both high-end shops and smaller boutiques. Visitors will also find a wide selection of souvenirs at the Bariloche Artisan Market, which takes place every weekend and features a wide variety of locally made goods.

If you're seeking unique gifts and souvenirs that reflect the essence of Patagonia, the markets and specialized shops in Bariloche are the perfect place to explore.

7.3 Markets and Local Shopping Centers

Bariloche has several markets and shopping centers where visitors can find everything from local handicrafts to international brands. Whether you're looking for traditional Argentine goods or modern retail experiences, Bariloche's shopping scene offers plenty of variety.

Feria Artesanal de Bariloche (Bariloche Artisan Market)

The Feria Artesanal is one of the most popular markets in the city and is located in the Centro Cívico area. The market takes place every weekend and features over 100 artisan stalls selling a variety of handcrafted products. Here, you can find everything from wooden carvings and leather goods to jewelry, textiles, and paintings.

The Feria Artesanal is a great place to purchase unique, one-of-a-kind items directly from the artisans. Many of the products sold at the market are made using traditional techniques that have been passed down through generations, making them both culturally significant and high-quality.

Mercado Municipal de Bariloche

The Mercado Municipal (Municipal Market) is another popular spot for those looking to buy local produce, meats, cheeses, and handcrafted goods. The market is a hub for both locals and tourists, offering a wide range of fresh produce, local delicacies, and traditional Argentine products. In addition to food and crafts, the Mercado Municipal also features several stands selling textiles, jewelry, and leather goods.

For those interested in the culinary side of Bariloche, the market is a fantastic place to find regional ingredients such as smoked meats, cheeses, and traditional baked goods. The local cheeses, in particular, are worth trying, as Patagonia is known for its high-quality dairy products.

Shopping Centers

For more conventional shopping experiences, Bariloche also has several shopping centers where visitors can find both local and international brands. One of the largest shopping centers is Shopping Patagonia, which is located on the outskirts of the city. This modern mall features a wide range of shops, from clothing and electronics to home goods and cosmetics.

Another shopping option is La Plaza Shopping, which is a more boutique-style shopping center located in the city center. Here, you'll find a selection of local boutiques, high-end clothing shops, and specialty stores, along with a few cafes and restaurants where you can relax after a day of shopping.

Shopping in Bariloche is an experience that goes beyond buying souvenirs—it's an opportunity to immerse yourself in the culture and artistry of Patagonia. From handcrafted goods made by local artisans to the world-renowned chocolates, wines, and crafts that the region is known for, Bariloche offers a shopping experience that is as varied and beautiful as its landscapes. Whether you're searching for a unique gift, indulging in local delicacies, or simply exploring the city's markets and shops, Bariloche has something for every type of shopper.

Chapter 8: Adventure Sports and Activities

Bariloche, Argentina, nestled in the stunning Patagonia region, offers a wealth of adventure sports and activities, making it one of the top destinations for outdoor enthusiasts. From adrenaline-pumping experiences like paragliding and fly fishing to off-roading and winter sports, Bariloche provides countless opportunities to immerse yourself in the region's natural beauty. Whether you're seeking thrilling adventure or simply looking to connect with nature, the diverse landscape of Bariloche is sure to offer an unforgettable experience.

8.1 Paragliding and Adventure Tours

Paragliding is one of the most popular and exhilarating activities that Bariloche offers. Flying through the skies, soaring above the crystal-clear lakes and snow-capped mountains, provides a unique perspective of the region's breathtaking beauty. It's an adventure that combines adrenaline, nature, and the feeling of freedom that only flight can bring.

Paragliding in Bariloche

Bariloche's natural landscapes provide the perfect setting for paragliding. The area's topography, with its combination of lakes, mountains, and forests, offers the ideal conditions for paragliding flights. Most paragliding activities are concentrated around the hills of Cerro Otto and Cerro Campanario. Both offer stunning views of the town, Nahuel Huapi Lake, and the Andes mountains, making these the prime locations for paragliding.

Tandem Paragliding Flights:

For those without prior experience, tandem paragliding is a fantastic option. Tandem flights allow you to soar high above the landscapes with an experienced instructor. The thrill of being airborne while taking in the panoramic views of the surrounding natural beauty is an experience that will stay with you long after your feet are back on solid ground.

The tandem flights typically last around 15 to 30 minutes, depending on weather conditions, and offer a bird's-eye view of Bariloche and its surroundings. As you glide through the air, you'll have the chance to spot the city below, the expanse of Nahuel Huapi Lake, and the towering peaks of the Andes. The experience is as much about the serenity of the flight as it is about the thrill.

Adventure Tours in Bariloche

For those seeking more than just a taste of adventure, Bariloche offers a wide variety of adventure tours. These tours can combine several activities in one day or extend over several days, allowing you to explore Patagonia's wilderness in a guided and safe manner. Some of the most popular adventure tours in Bariloche include:

- **Hiking and Trekking Tours:** Bariloche's diverse landscape makes it a prime destination for hiking and trekking tours. Guided tours take visitors to some of the most scenic spots around the city, including hidden valleys, high-altitude lakes, and ancient forests. These tours can be customized based on your fitness level and preferred length of trek.

- **Mountain Biking Tours:** Bariloche's rugged terrain is perfect for mountain biking. Whether you're a beginner or an experienced rider, there are various routes available that take you through picturesque landscapes, such as the popular Circuito Chico, which offers incredible views of the surrounding lakes and mountains.

- **Kayaking and Canoeing Tours:** Kayaking on Nahuel Huapi Lake is a fantastic way to explore the pristine waters of the lake while surrounded by the breathtaking scenery of the Andes. Guided kayaking tours allow you to paddle through calm waters, visit remote beaches, and explore islands that are otherwise inaccessible.

- **Snowmobile and Off-Road Tours:** During winter, visitors can enjoy snowmobile tours that take them into the snowy wilderness of Patagonia. These tours typically include an adrenaline-filled ride across snowy trails with panoramic views of the mountains.

8.2 Fly Fishing and Water Activities

Bariloche, located on the shores of Nahuel Huapi Lake, is a premier destination for fishing enthusiasts. Known for its pristine waters, the lake, along with the many rivers in the area, provides excellent opportunities for fly fishing, as well as a variety of water-based activities such as kayaking and sailing.

Fly Fishing in Bariloche

Fly fishing is a particularly popular activity in the region, thanks to the abundance of fish in the lakes and rivers. The rivers that feed into Nahuel Huapi Lake, such as the Limay and Traful Rivers, are known for their populations of brown trout, rainbow trout, and brook trout. Fly fishing in these crystal-clear waters offers not only an exciting challenge but also a serene connection with nature.

Best Fly Fishing Spots in Bariloche:

- **Limay River:** Known for its large trout, the Limay River is one of the most sought-after fly fishing spots in the region. The river offers both calm and fast-moving sections, making it ideal for different fishing techniques. The Limay is also less crowded than some of the other areas, providing a more tranquil fishing experience.

- **Traful River:** This river is known for its beautiful surroundings and excellent fishing opportunities. The Traful River runs through dense forests and offers many peaceful spots for anglers to enjoy. The crystal-clear waters make it easy to spot fish, and the abundance of wildlife adds to the tranquil experience.

- **Nahuel Huapi Lake:** Fishing in Nahuel Huapi Lake is another fantastic option, particularly for those looking to catch larger fish like rainbow trout and lake trout. The lake's size and its relatively remote nature provide an opportunity for a quiet day of fishing with stunning views.

Guided Fly Fishing Tours:

For those new to fly fishing or who want to maximize their chances of success, guided fly fishing tours are available. These tours are led by experienced local guides who know the best fishing spots and can provide valuable tips on techniques. The guides also have the necessary equipment for fishing, including rods, flies, and waders, so you can enjoy the experience without worrying about bringing your own gear.

Other Water Activities

In addition to fly fishing, Bariloche offers a variety of other water activities for those who prefer to stay on the water's surface.

- **Kayaking and Canoeing:** Kayaking is one of the best ways to experience the calm and beauty of Nahuel Huapi Lake. There are various kayaking tours that take visitors around the lake, exploring hidden coves, secluded beaches, and islands. These tours are suitable for beginners and more experienced paddlers.

- **Sailing:** Nahuel Huapi Lake is large enough to enjoy sailing, and many companies offer sailboat rentals or guided sailing tours. Sailing allows you to relax on the calm waters while taking in the magnificent surroundings. Whether you prefer a quiet day of relaxation or a more exhilarating sailing experience, there are options for every type of sailor.

- **Stand-Up Paddleboarding (SUP):** Stand-up paddleboarding is another popular activity in Bariloche, especially on the calmer sections of Nahuel Huapi Lake. It's an excellent way to enjoy the lake's beauty while getting some light exercise. SUP rentals are available, and there are several guided tours for beginners.

8.3 Winter Sports Beyond Skiing

While skiing and snowboarding are undoubtedly the stars of winter sports in Bariloche, the region offers much more in terms of cold-weather activities. The surrounding mountains, forests, and lakes provide ample opportunities for adventure seekers looking for something different.

Snowshoeing

Snowshoeing is a popular winter activity in Bariloche, allowing visitors to explore the snow-covered forests and mountains without the need for specialized equipment like skis. Snowshoes allow you to walk over deep snow, making it easy to access areas that would otherwise be difficult to reach in winter. Snowshoeing tours are available for all skill levels, from gentle walks in the forest to more challenging treks to higher altitudes.

The views during a snowshoeing excursion are some of the most beautiful in Patagonia, with towering snow-capped peaks, frozen lakes, and dense forests. Many snowshoeing tours are guided, and guides provide all the necessary equipment and safety instructions to ensure a safe and enjoyable experience.

Snowmobiling

For those who crave speed and excitement, snowmobiling is an exhilarating way to explore the snowy landscapes around Bariloche. Snowmobile tours are available that take you through the Patagonian wilderness, covering vast areas of snowy terrain. Snowmobiling is a great way to reach more remote and pristine areas of the region, where you can enjoy breathtaking views of mountains and lakes.

These tours are led by experienced guides, and the equipment is provided. Snowmobiling is a thrilling way to experience the winter wonderland of Bariloche, especially for those who enjoy an adrenaline rush.

Ice Climbing

For adventurous souls seeking a more extreme winter sport, ice climbing is a unique and challenging activity available in the Bariloche region. The frozen waterfalls and ice-covered rock formations in the area provide perfect opportunities for this adrenaline-fueled activity. Professional guides lead ice climbing tours, ensuring that safety is always a priority. Beginners and more advanced climbers alike can enjoy the challenge of scaling frozen waterfalls while taking in the spectacular winter scenery.

8.4 Off-Roading and 4x4 Adventures

Bariloche is an ideal location for off-roading and 4x4 adventures, thanks to its diverse terrain and rugged landscapes. Whether you want to explore dense forests, traverse rocky paths, or drive up steep mountain roads, Bariloche offers an incredible variety of off-roading experiences.

4x4 Tours in Bariloche

Several companies offer 4x4 tours that take visitors off the beaten path to explore Bariloche's most remote and beautiful areas. These guided tours typically use specially equipped vehicles designed for rough terrain, allowing visitors to reach areas that are otherwise inaccessible by regular cars.

Popular 4x4 Adventure Routes:

- **Cerro Otto and Cerro Campanario:** These areas are known for their spectacular views and rugged terrain. 4x4 tours can take visitors to the summits of these hills, where they can enjoy panoramic views of Bariloche and its surrounding landscapes. The tours typically include stops at scenic viewpoints and offer opportunities for short hikes to further explore the area.

- **Laguna El Trébol:** This off-road route takes visitors to one of Bariloche's lesser-known yet stunning lakes. The journey to Laguna El Trébol is an adventure in itself, as it involves traversing dirt roads and rocky paths that require 4x4 vehicles to navigate. Once at the lake, visitors can enjoy the tranquility of the area, often with the opportunity for a picnic or a swim.

- **Lake Gutierrez and Surrounding Areas:** For those seeking a full-day off-road adventure, tours around Lake Gutierrez offer a chance to explore the diverse landscapes of Patagonia. These routes often take visitors through forests, along the lake's shores, and up into the mountains, providing an unforgettable adventure with the chance to see wildlife and pristine nature.

Off-Roading for Wildlife Watching

Bariloche's off-road tours are also a fantastic way to experience wildlife. The region is home to diverse animals, including deer, wild boars, foxes, and a variety of bird species. Off-road tours often incorporate wildlife watching, giving you the opportunity to spot animals in their natural habitats.

Bariloche's adventure sports and activities offer something for every thrill-seeker. From soaring through the skies with paragliding to exploring Patagonia's rugged landscapes in a 4x4 vehicle, there are countless ways to experience the beauty of the region. Whether you're kayaking on Nahuel Huapi Lake, fishing for trout, or hitting the slopes, Bariloche's outdoor adventures provide an unparalleled opportunity to connect with nature and create unforgettable memories.

Chapter 9: Family-Friendly Activities

Bariloche, a stunning city in the Argentine Patagonia region, offers a variety of family-friendly activities that will make your visit memorable for everyone, from toddlers to grandparents. With its stunning natural surroundings, wildlife, and wide range of outdoor and indoor attractions, Bariloche provides families with endless opportunities to explore, learn, and have fun together. In this chapter, we will delve into the many family-friendly activities Bariloche has to offer, including kid-friendly nature walks, parks and playgrounds, cultural experiences, and exciting adventures at Cerro Otto.

9.1 Kid-Friendly Trails and Nature Walks

One of the best ways to immerse your family in the natural beauty of Bariloche is by exploring its many trails and nature walks. The city and its surroundings are filled with accessible paths that are suitable for families with children. These trails offer the perfect blend of adventure, exercise, and the chance to witness some of Patagonia's most spectacular landscapes.

Circuito Chico

The Circuito Chico is a well-known scenic route that stretches around the outskirts of Bariloche. While it is often driven by tourists seeking stunning views, the Circuito Chico also offers easy, family-friendly hiking opportunities. The entire route is around 27 kilometers long, but you don't need to tackle the whole circuit to enjoy it. Several short trails along the way provide incredible views of the surrounding lakes and mountains, and there are plenty of spots for picnicking or just relaxing. This is a great trail for children, as it's not too difficult and offers a chance to spot local wildlife like birds, rabbits, and even the occasional deer.

Lago Gutierrez Trail

If your family is looking for a gentle nature walk with beautiful views, the Lago Gutierrez trail is a wonderful option. This easy-to-follow trail is around 5 kilometers in total, making it perfect for families with children of all ages. The path runs along the edge of Lake Gutierrez, offering tranquil views of the crystal-clear water and the surrounding forested hills. It's a peaceful, serene walk, ideal for younger children to enjoy without the strain of a more challenging hike. Along the way, families can enjoy the sights of birds and other local wildlife, making it a great opportunity for kids to learn about the flora and fauna of Patagonia.

Refugio Frey Hike (For Older Kids)

For families with older children or teenagers who are eager for a more challenging adventure, the hike to Refugio Frey is an excellent option. This 7-hour hike takes visitors to an alpine refuge located at the base of a dramatic rock spire, surrounded by pristine lakes and high mountains. While this trail is more difficult than the others mentioned, it is well worth the effort, and kids with a sense of adventure will relish the challenge. Along the way, there are opportunities to explore wild forests and observe Patagonian wildlife. It's a great way for older kids and teens to connect with nature while pushing themselves physically.

Short Trails Around Cerro Campanario

Another kid-friendly trail that provides fantastic views of Bariloche and the surrounding landscapes is the hike to Cerro Campanario. This relatively short walk leads visitors to a viewpoint at the top of the mountain, where panoramic views of Lake Nahuel Huapi, the surrounding forests, and the snow-capped peaks of the Andes await. The trail is short but offers enough of a challenge to engage children and provide them with a sense of accomplishment. For families who prefer not to hike, there is also a chairlift that can take you to the top of the hill, where you can still enjoy the breathtaking views without the hike.

9.2 Parks and Playgrounds

Bariloche has several parks and playgrounds that provide perfect spots for families to relax and children to play. These green spaces are an excellent way to take a break from more intense activities while still enjoying the beauty of nature.

Parque Nahuel Huapi

Parque Nahuel Huapi is Bariloche's largest and most important national park, offering families the chance to enjoy nature, wildlife, and relaxation all in one place. The park stretches for over 7,000 square kilometers, offering vast forests, mountain lakes, and a wide range of outdoor activities for families. For families with children, there are several easily accessible walking trails, along with open spaces for picnics and play. The park is a great place to explore, with the opportunity to spot local wildlife such as deer, rabbits, and various bird species.

Within the park, there are many areas that are ideal for younger children to run around and explore. The park's proximity to Bariloche also makes it easy for families to visit during their stay. Whether you're looking to relax, have a picnic, or simply wander the grounds, Parque Nahuel Huapi provides the perfect family escape into nature.

Playa Bonita

If your family enjoys spending time by the water, Playa Bonita is an excellent spot for both relaxation and fun. Located just a short drive from the city center, this popular lakeside park is perfect for a day out with kids. The beach offers gentle, shallow waters ideal for younger children to swim and wade in. There are also grassy areas where families can lay out blankets, have a picnic, or play games. In addition to its relaxed atmosphere, Playa Bonita provides a wonderful backdrop of the surrounding mountains and forests, making it an ideal location for family photos.

Parque Los Pioneros

For families looking for a more structured play area, Parque Los Pioneros is a park that offers both playgrounds and educational exhibits about Bariloche's history and culture. The park's playgrounds feature slides, swings, and climbing structures, making it a perfect place for younger children to burn off energy. It's a family-friendly space where parents can relax while their kids explore the various play areas. Additionally, the park often hosts local cultural events, adding an educational element to the visit.

9.3 Educational Experiences: Museums and Cultural Tours

Bariloche offers several educational experiences for families, where children and adults alike can learn about the region's history, wildlife, and culture. These museums and cultural attractions provide both fun and educational value, making them perfect for a family day out.

Museo de la Patagonia

Located in Bariloche's Civic Center, the Museo de la Patagonia (Museum of Patagonia) offers a fascinating insight into the region's history, from its geological formation to its indigenous cultures and wildlife. The museum is an excellent educational experience for families, featuring exhibits on Patagonia's natural history, including fossils, minerals, and animal specimens. The museum's interactive exhibits are engaging for children, and the displays are designed to educate visitors about the unique environment of the region.

One of the museum's highlights is its section dedicated to Patagonia's indigenous peoples, which features artifacts, tools, and displays about the cultures that have lived in the region for thousands of years. Families can spend hours exploring the museum, making it a perfect rainy-day activity.

Centro Cívico and the Historic Center of Bariloche

For families interested in learning more about Bariloche's history, the Centro Cívico (Civic Center) and the historic center of the city offer fascinating educational experiences. The Civic Center is an architectural landmark, and it houses a variety of cultural institutions, including local art galleries and museums. Families can take a walking tour of the area to learn about the city's foundation, the development of its tourism industry, and its evolution over the years.

In addition to the Civic Center, walking around the town's historic streets will give visitors the chance to admire the unique alpine-style architecture that was brought by European immigrants, particularly Swiss and German settlers. Many of these immigrants contributed to the development of the city's culture, and learning about their influence is an enriching experience for all ages.

The Patagonia Wildlife Rescue Center

Another great educational experience for families is a visit to the Patagonia Wildlife Rescue Center. This center focuses on the rehabilitation and protection of local wildlife, such as deer, foxes, and birds of prey. The center offers guided tours that teach visitors about the importance of wildlife conservation and the challenges that animals in Patagonia face. Kids will be fascinated by the animals and learn valuable lessons about the environment and the efforts to protect endangered species. The center also offers opportunities to get involved in conservation efforts through volunteering or making donations.

9.4 Fun at Cerro Otto and the Indoor Amusement Park

Bariloche's **Cerro Otto** is a fantastic destination for families, offering not only stunning views of the surrounding landscape but also an array of fun activities for children.

The Cerro Otto Cable Car

One of the best ways to reach the top of Cerro Otto is by taking the Cerro Otto Cable Car. The cable car ride offers spectacular views of the city, Nahuel Huapi Lake, and the snow-capped Andes. Children will love the experience of soaring above the trees and enjoying the ride, and once at the top, they can explore the viewing platforms and enjoy the 360-degree panoramic views of the surrounding areas.

Indoor Amusement Park at Cerro Otto

At the summit of Cerro Otto, you'll find an indoor amusement park that is perfect for younger children. The amusement park features a variety of fun rides and games that will keep kids entertained for hours. There are small carousels, video games, and even a few interactive exhibits that combine fun with learning. The indoor amusement park is a great way to keep kids engaged and happy, especially on a cloudy or rainy day. Additionally, the amusement park has a café where parents can relax while their children enjoy the attractions.

Hiking and Scenic Exploration

For families looking for more active outdoor fun, Cerro Otto also offers easy-to-moderate hiking trails that lead to beautiful viewpoints. Kids will enjoy exploring the natural surroundings, and the hikes are relatively short, making them suitable for families with young children.

Bariloche offers a wide variety of family-friendly activities that will appeal to children and adults alike. Whether you're hiking the kid-friendly trails around the lakes, exploring the interactive museums, or enjoying the fun indoor amusement park at Cerro Otto, there's no shortage of opportunities for families to bond while exploring the natural beauty and cultural richness of Patagonia. With its mix of outdoor adventures, educational experiences, and playful activities, Bariloche is the ideal destination for families seeking a memorable vacation in Argentina.

Chapter 10: Bariloche for Nature Lovers

Bariloche, located in Argentina's stunning Patagonia region, is a paradise for nature lovers. Surrounded by snow-capped mountains, crystal-clear lakes, dense forests, and a rich diversity of wildlife, Bariloche offers an unparalleled opportunity to explore the natural world. Whether you are a wildlife enthusiast, a birdwatcher, or simply someone who appreciates the beauty of the great outdoors, Bariloche's natural attractions will captivate you. In this chapter, we'll explore some of the best wildlife and bird-watching experiences, national parks and protected areas, as well as botanical gardens and nature reserves that make Bariloche a must-visit destination for anyone passionate about nature.

10.1 Wildlife Watching and Bird Watching

Bariloche is home to an incredibly diverse range of wildlife, thanks to its varied landscapes and unique ecological zones. From the towering Andes to the expansive forests and pristine lakes, the region is a haven for wildlife enthusiasts. Whether you are trekking through forests, exploring the lakesides, or simply observing from a distance, Bariloche offers many opportunities for wildlife watching.

Mammals of Bariloche

Bariloche's wildlife includes a variety of mammal species, many of which are well adapted to the region's diverse climates and terrains. Some of the most commonly spotted mammals in the Bariloche area include:

- **Andean Deer (Huemul):** The huemul is one of the most iconic and endangered animals of Patagonia. This shy, medium-sized deer is found in the high-altitude regions of the Andes, including parts of Bariloche. Spotting a huemul is a rare and special experience, and visitors who are passionate about conservation will appreciate the opportunity to see this majestic animal in its natural habitat. Guided tours are available that focus on finding these elusive deer in protected areas like **Nahuel Huapi National Park**.

- **Puma:** The puma, or mountain lion, is another elusive predator that roams the mountains and forests of Bariloche. While sightings are rare due to their solitary nature and nocturnal habits, local guides can share information about puma behavior and help visitors track their movements, providing a thrilling experience for wildlife enthusiasts.

- **Coypu (Nutria):** The coypu, also known as nutria, is a large rodent native to the region. Often found along the shores of lakes and rivers, these animals are semi-aquatic and can be seen foraging along the banks of **Nahuel Huapi Lake** and other nearby bodies of water. Though not as elusive as some of the larger mammals, they offer a chance to observe more active wildlife while walking along trails or visiting beaches.

- **Red Fox:** The red fox is a common sight in the forests and grasslands around Bariloche. Known for its adaptability, the red fox is often seen hunting small mammals, birds, and insects. Foxes are particularly active at dawn and dusk, making these times the best for spotting them.

Bird Watching in Bariloche

Bariloche's diverse ecosystems make it an excellent location for birdwatching. The region's forests, lakes, rivers, and wetlands provide habitats for a wide variety of bird species, both migratory and resident. Birdwatching enthusiasts will find numerous opportunities to observe unique species of birds, many of which are not found in other parts of the world.

- **Andean Condor:** The Andean condor, one of the largest flying birds in the world, is a highlight for birdwatchers visiting Bariloche. With a wingspan of up to 3 meters, this majestic bird is often spotted soaring high above the Andes mountains, looking for thermals to glide on. These birds are a common sight around **Cerro Tronador** and **Cerro Campanario**, where they can be seen from elevated viewpoints.

- **Magellanic Woodpecker:** The Magellanic woodpecker is another stunning bird that can be found in the forests of Bariloche. This large woodpecker, with its striking red head and black body, is a forest dweller that makes its home in the dense Patagonian forests. The best time to spot them is during the spring and summer months when they are most active.

- **Black-necked Swan:** This beautiful waterfowl can be found on the calm, shallow waters of Bariloche's lakes, particularly Lago Moreno. The black-necked swan has distinctive black and white plumage, and sightings of them are especially common during the colder months when they congregate in larger flocks.

- **Rufous-tailed Plantcutter:** A small, colorful bird native to Patagonia, the Rufous-tailed plantcutter can be spotted in the grassy areas around Bariloche. The bird is known for its distinctive rufous tail and its song, which it uses to communicate with other members of its species.

- **Southern Lapwing:** This large, ground-dwelling bird can be found near lakes and wetlands in Bariloche. The Southern Lapwing is known for its bold behavior and striking black-and-white plumage. These birds are particularly common around the edges of Nahuel Huapi Lake and the wetlands surrounding Lake Gutierrez.

Guided Wildlife Tours

To make the most of your wildlife-watching experience, consider taking a guided tour. Local naturalists and wildlife experts can provide valuable insight into the region's ecosystems and help you spot more elusive species. Guided wildlife tours are available in many areas around Bariloche, including Nahuel Huapi National Park and Los Alerces National Park, and can be customized based on your specific interests, such as mammal watching, bird watching, or photography.

10.2 National Parks and Protected Areas

Bariloche is home to several national parks and protected areas that serve as refuges for wildlife and provide visitors with the opportunity to explore some of the most pristine and unspoiled landscapes in the world. These parks and protected areas are vital for conservation and provide unparalleled opportunities for outdoor recreation.

Nahuel Huapi National Park

Nahuel Huapi National Park is one of Argentina's oldest and largest national parks, covering more than 7,000 square kilometers. Located around Bariloche and extending into Chile, the park is a UNESCO Biosphere Reserve and one of the most important protected areas in Patagonia. The park encompasses a variety of ecosystems, including forests, wetlands, and alpine regions, making it a biodiversity hotspot.

- **Hiking and Trekking:** Nahuel Huapi National Park offers numerous hiking trails, ranging from easy walks to challenging multi-day treks. Popular trails like the hike to Refugio Frey offer incredible views of the surrounding peaks and provide a chance to experience the park's diverse flora and fauna.

- **Wildlife:** The park is home to an array of wildlife, including the endangered huemul deer, pumas, guanacos, and numerous bird species. Birdwatchers will find the park particularly appealing, as it is home to many species of ducks, geese, and other waterfowl, as well as forest birds like the Magellanic woodpecker.

- **Lakes and Rivers:** The park's many lakes, including Nahuel Huapi Lake, Lake Moreno, and Lake Gutiérrez, are perfect for water activities like kayaking, fishing, and boating. The lakes also provide habitats for various fish species and waterfowl, adding to the park's ecological richness.

Los Alerces National Park

Located to the north of Bariloche, Los Alerces National Park is another incredible destination for nature lovers. This park is famous for its ancient forests of alerce trees, some of which are over 3,000 years old. The park is also home to pristine lakes, rivers, and glaciers, making it a stunning location for hiking, boating, and wildlife watching.

- **Alerce Trees:** The park's alerce trees are among the oldest and most massive living organisms on Earth. Visitors can explore the Alerce Milenario (Ancient Alerce) trail, where they can see some of the park's oldest trees, which have survived for thousands of years.

- **Hiking and Trekking:** Los Alerces offers a range of hiking trails, including routes around its crystal-clear lakes and through dense forests. The Lake Futalaufquen area is particularly popular, with trails that offer views of the surrounding mountains and glaciers.

- **Wildlife and Bird Watching:** The park is home to a variety of wildlife, including guanacos, red deer, and wild boar. It is also a great spot for birdwatching, with species like the Andean condor, Chilean flamingo, and various species of ducks and geese frequenting the lakes and rivers.

Lanín National Park

Situated to the north of Bariloche, Lanín National Park is another prominent natural reserve in Patagonia. The park is known for its towering pine forests, clear rivers, and impressive peaks, makin1g it a perfect destination for hiking, camping, and outdoor adventures.

- **Hiking and Mountaineering:** The park offers numerous trails that lead to spectacular viewpoints, such as Lake Alumine and the Lanín Volcano. These trails are perfect for families, nature lovers, and experienced trekkers alike.

- **Wildlife:** Lanín National Park is home to a diverse range of wildlife, including native species like the Andean fox, deer, and the endangered huemul. The park's rich ecosystems support a variety of birdlife as well, making it a favorite destination for birdwatchers.

- **Fishing and Canoeing:** The park's rivers and lakes provide excellent opportunities for fishing, particularly for trout. Visitors can also enjoy canoeing on the park's serene lakes, including Lake Huechulafquen, a popular spot for water sports.

10.3 Botanical Gardens and Nature Reserves

In addition to the expansive national parks and wildlife reserves, Bariloche is home to several botanical gardens and nature reserves that showcase the region's unique plant life. These areas are perfect for anyone interested in learning more about the local flora and enjoying the beauty of nature in a more contained, peaceful environment.

Patagonia's Botanical Garden

Bariloche's Patagonia's Botanical Garden is an excellent place to explore the native flora of the region. Located just outside the city, the botanical garden covers a wide variety of ecosystems, from alpine meadows to dense forests, and is dedicated to preserving the region's native plants.

- **Educational Displays:** The garden offers educational exhibits that explain the importance of native plants and their role in the local ecosystem. Families and nature enthusiasts will enjoy walking through the garden's paths, where they can observe and learn about various plant species, including the coihue tree, ñire, and lenga.

- **Specialized Gardens:** The garden also features specialized areas dedicated to particular plant types, including medicinal plants and alpine species. These areas provide a deeper understanding of how these plants have adapted to the harsh Patagonian environment.

Huella Andina Nature Reserve

The Huella Andina is a protected natural reserve located near Bariloche, offering visitors the chance to explore untouched forests, lakes, and rivers. The reserve is particularly noted for its conservation efforts to protect the region's biodiversity and for its hiking trails that offer beautiful vistas of the surrounding landscape.

- **Conservation Efforts:** The reserve plays an important role in protecting Patagonian plant and animal species, including native trees like the Andean cypress and alder. It's an ideal destination for nature lovers looking to explore Patagonia's wilderness and contribute to conservation efforts.

- **Hiking Trails:** The reserve offers several trails for hiking, including routes that pass through forests of native species and lead to scenic viewpoints. The trails are suitable for all levels of hikers, making this a great spot for families to explore together.

Bariloche offers nature lovers an abundance of opportunities to explore its pristine landscapes, rich wildlife, and diverse ecosystems. From wildlife watching and birding to hiking through national parks and protected areas, the region's natural beauty is a constant source of awe and inspiration. Whether you're wandering through ancient forests of alerce trees, spotting rare birds soaring over the Andes, or relaxing in a botanical garden surrounded by the flora of Patagonia, Bariloche offers an unforgettable experience for all who seek to connect with the natural world.

Chapter 11: Nightlife and Entertainment

Bariloche, located in the Argentine Patagonia region, is known for its stunning landscapes, outdoor adventures, and outdoor activities. However, when the sun sets and the cool Patagonian night embraces the city, Bariloche transforms into a lively hub for nightlife and entertainment. While the city is best known for its natural beauty, it also offers a variety of bars, pubs, nightclubs, live music, and cultural performances. In this chapter, we will explore Bariloche's vibrant nightlife, from trendy bars and nightclubs to live music venues and local festivals, ensuring that there's something for everyone, whether you seek a relaxed night out or a more energetic and immersive experience.

11.1 Bars, Pubs, and Nightclubs

Bariloche offers a diverse range of drinking establishments, from casual pubs with local craft beers to upscale cocktail bars and energetic nightclubs. The nightlife scene in Bariloche is relaxed but vibrant, catering to a variety of tastes and preferences. Whether you're looking to enjoy a quiet drink with scenic views or dance the night away, Bariloche's bars and nightclubs offer something for everyone.

Bars and Pubs

Bariloche is home to several cozy bars and lively pubs where you can enjoy a drink, socialize with locals, and unwind after a day of exploring. The Civic Center area, which is the heart of the city, is home to many of Bariloche's best bars and pubs. Many of these establishments feature large selections of Argentine wines, local craft beers, and signature cocktails, perfect for an evening out.

- **La Costa del Pueblo:** This relaxed bar and pub is a popular gathering spot for locals and tourists alike. It's known for its welcoming atmosphere, with a variety of Argentine craft beers on tap and a small menu of Argentine snacks, such as empanadas and choripán (sausage sandwiches). The cozy setting makes it a great place to start the evening with a drink in hand and enjoy some casual conversation.

- **El Boliche de Alberto:** While El Boliche de Alberto is primarily known for its delicious asado (barbecue), it also has a full bar and is a popular destination for a lively evening out. The pub's rustic and warm ambiance, combined with its delicious food and drinks, makes it a great choice for those looking to enjoy a more relaxed but vibrant atmosphere.

- **Cervecería La Cruz:** Known for its variety of craft beers brewed locally, Cervecería La Cruz is a favorite among beer lovers. The pub offers a wide range of Argentine beers, with several options from Patagonia's own breweries. The laid-back atmosphere, combined with delicious beers and local snacks, makes it an ideal location for a casual night out.

- **Tijuana Bar:** A trendy bar located near the city center, Tijuana Bar is known for its extensive cocktail menu and modern vibe. It has become a popular spot for those looking for a chic and fun place to enjoy drinks and socialize. The bar's mixologists are skilled at crafting creative cocktails, and it frequently hosts themed nights and events to keep the atmosphere fresh and exciting.

Nightclubs

For those who want to dance the night away, Bariloche has a selection of nightclubs that offer a lively atmosphere and upbeat music. The city's nightclubs feature everything from electronic dance music (EDM) to Latin rhythms, creating a diverse nightlife scene that caters to different tastes.

- **ByPass Bariloche:** ByPass is one of the most popular nightclubs in Bariloche, known for its energetic atmosphere and vibrant music scene. The club features a variety of music styles, from international electronic music to local Latin and rock bands. It has multiple rooms and areas for dancing and socializing, with both indoor and outdoor spaces where you can enjoy the cool Patagonian night air.

- **Tetris Bar:** If you're in the mood for a lively night of dancing, Tetris Bar is another top destination in Bariloche. This nightclub is famous for its vibrant atmosphere, music ranging from EDM to reggaeton, and great drink specials. It's a fun place to mingle with locals and fellow travelers while enjoying music that keeps the party going into the early morning hours.

- **La Casita de Papel:** Located slightly off the beaten path, La Casita de Papel is a nightclub that specializes in providing a unique experience with a mix of indie, rock, and alternative music. It's a great option for those who prefer a more intimate atmosphere while still enjoying the excitement of a nightclub. The venue often hosts live DJ sets, making it a popular place for Bariloche's younger crowd to gather.

Enjoying the Nightlife in Bariloche

While Bariloche is not known for the same kind of party scene you might find in larger cities like Buenos Aires or Mendoza, it offers a relaxed yet lively nightlife experience. Whether you're looking to sample local wines at a cozy bar, enjoy a craft beer at a local pub, or dance until dawn at a nightclub, Bariloche's nightlife scene will offer something to suit your mood.

Many bars and pubs in Bariloche have outdoor terraces with incredible views of the surrounding lakes and mountains, providing a scenic backdrop for a quiet evening. For those looking for a more energetic experience, the city's nightclubs offer an upbeat atmosphere, where you can dance to a wide range of music and mingle with locals and fellow travelers.

11.2 Live Music and Events

Bariloche has a thriving live music scene, with performances happening in bars, pubs, cultural centers, and even outdoor venues during the warmer months. The city attracts both local and international musicians, and there is something for every musical taste, from jazz and rock to folk and tango.

Local Music Scene

Bariloche has a rich musical heritage, with influences ranging from Argentine folk to international rock and electronic music. Many local venues host live music performances, giving visitors a chance to enjoy a variety of genres and experience the culture of the city. Some of the most well-known venues for live music include:

- **El Viejo Marino:** Located along the waterfront with a beautiful view of the lake, El Viejo Marino is a bar and restaurant that regularly features live music performances. The venue hosts local folk, rock, and acoustic performances, offering a relaxed atmosphere where you can enjoy a meal or drink while listening to talented musicians.

- **La Balsa Bar:** Known for its cozy ambiance, La Balsa is a popular spot for intimate live music performances. The venue hosts local musicians and bands, showcasing a variety of genres, including rock, folk, jazz, and tango. The laid-back vibe, combined with quality performances, makes it a favorite among locals and tourists alike.

- **La Casa de la Historia y la Cultura del Bicentenario:** This cultural center often hosts live music performances, including classical, jazz, and folkloric music. It's an excellent spot for those interested in experiencing the cultural richness of Argentina while enjoying beautiful live performances in an intimate setting.

Music Festivals

Bariloche is also home to a variety of music festivals that take place throughout the year, attracting both locals and international visitors. These festivals celebrate the diverse musical styles of the region and provide a platform for talented artists to showcase their work.

- **Festival de la Noche de los Museos (Night of the Museums Festival):** This annual festival is held in Bariloche's historic cultural venues, and it features a range of live music performances, from jazz to folk. The event provides a unique opportunity to explore Bariloche's museums and cultural centers while enjoying performances by talented local musicians.

- **Patagonia Jazz Festival:** A celebrated event in the city, the Patagonia Jazz Festival brings international and local jazz musicians to Bariloche for a week of live performances. The festival attracts jazz lovers from across the region and features performances in a variety of venues, including open-air concerts and intimate club settings.

- **Fiesta Nacional de la Nieve** (National Snow Festival): Bariloche's National Snow Festival is a celebration of winter, featuring not only snow-related activities but also live music performances. The festival includes everything from local tango bands to international rock concerts, giving visitors the chance to enjoy a wide variety of musical performances alongside the festivities of the winter season.

11.3 Cultural Performances and Festivals

Bariloche is not just a destination for outdoor adventures, but also a city with a rich cultural life. From traditional Argentine music and dance to contemporary arts, the city offers numerous opportunities to experience the country's cultural heritage. Local festivals, performances, and cultural events are held throughout the year, showcasing the best of Patagonian traditions.

Tango and Folklore

Tango, a style of music and dance that is deeply ingrained in Argentine culture, is an essential part of Bariloche's cultural scene. There are several venues in the city that host tango shows, where visitors can watch talented dancers perform this passionate and expressive dance. Many venues also offer tango lessons for those who want to learn the basic steps and immerse themselves in Argentine culture.

- **La Peña de los Amigos:** This venue is a staple for anyone wanting to experience Argentine folklore and tango music. Local musicians and dancers perform traditional folk music and tango in an intimate setting. Visitors can enjoy a traditional meal while watching the performances, making it an immersive cultural experience.

Local Festivals

Bariloche's cultural calendar is packed with events that showcase the region's traditions, arts, and culinary offerings. These festivals are an excellent way to connect with the local community and experience the culture firsthand.

- **Fiesta Nacional de la Nieve (National Snow Festival):** As mentioned earlier, the Fiesta Nacional de la Nieve is one of the most important events in Bariloche, celebrating the winter season with music, dancing, and cultural performances. The festival includes parades, fireworks, and local artisanal markets, as well as live performances by Argentine musicians and dancers. It's a lively and colorful event that attracts visitors from all over the world.

- **Festival de la Palta (Avocado Festival):** A quirky local event that celebrates the region's culinary traditions, the Festival de la Palta is a fun and unique way to explore the flavors of Patagonia. The festival includes live music, dance performances, food tastings, and local artisan booths, all centered around the beloved avocado, which has become a symbol of the region's growing food scene.

- **Festival de la Trucha (Trout Festival):** Bariloche's lakes are home to some of Argentina's best trout fishing, and the Festival de la Trucha is a celebration of this delicious fish. The festival includes cooking competitions, tastings, and live performances, showcasing the region's culinary and musical culture.

Theatrical Performances and Arts

Bariloche also has a thriving theatrical and artistic community, with several venues dedicated to the performing arts. The city's **Teatro La Baita** is a prime location for theatrical performances, featuring a wide variety of shows, from local theater productions to visiting companies. The theater hosts plays, dance performances, and art exhibitions, making it a cultural hub for those interested in the performing arts.

Bariloche's nightlife and entertainment scene offers a diverse range of options for visitors, from relaxed bars and pubs to lively nightclubs, live music venues, and cultural festivals. Whether you're looking to enjoy a quiet evening in a cozy bar, dance to the latest hits at a nightclub, or immerse yourself in the local culture through live performances and festivals, Bariloche has something for everyone. The city's vibrant nightlife and cultural offerings complement its stunning natural beauty, making it a fantastic destination for travelers who want to experience both adventure and culture.:

Chapter 12: Day Trips from Bariloche

Bariloche, located in the heart of Argentina's Patagonia region, is surrounded by some of the most spectacular landscapes in the world. Whether you're an adventure seeker, a nature lover, or someone who enjoys exploring picturesque towns, Bariloche serves as an excellent base for day trips that provide a deeper insight into Patagonia's diverse beauty. From visiting charming nearby villages to crossing the Andes into Chile, Bariloche's strategic location makes it the perfect starting point for unforgettable excursions. In this chapter, we will explore some of the best day trips from Bariloche, including excursions to Villa La Angostura, crossing the Andes into Chile, exploring the Patagonian Lakes Region, and discovering the scenic beauty of the Ruta de los 7 Lagos.

12.1 Excursions to Villa La Angostura

Villa La Angostura, a quaint and picturesque village located approximately 80 kilometers (50 miles) north of Bariloche, is one of the most popular day trip destinations. Situated on the shores of Lake Nahuel Huapi, Villa La Angostura is a hidden gem known for its stunning landscapes, charming atmosphere, and proximity to Los Arrayanes National Park. The town is an ideal escape for those who want to experience the tranquility of a small Patagonian village while still enjoying access to some incredible natural sites.

Scenic Drive to Villa La Angostura

The drive from Bariloche to Villa La Angostura is a beautiful journey through Patagonia's forests and mountains. The route follows Route 40, one of Argentina's most famous highways, offering stunning views of the surrounding lakes and forests. Along the way, you'll pass through the Llao Llao Peninsula, which is famous for its alpine-style architecture and lush forests.

As you approach Villa La Angostura, the views of Lake Nahuel Huapi become even more mesmerizing. The lake's deep blue waters reflect the snow-capped peaks of the Andes, creating a truly magical sight. This scenic drive alone makes the trip worthwhile, as you'll be able to immerse yourself in Patagonia's breathtaking beauty.

Villa La Angostura's Charm

Once you arrive in Villa La Angostura, you will be enchanted by its charming atmosphere. The town, known for its Swiss-style chalets and mountain views, has a laid-back, welcoming vibe. The main street, Av. Arrayanes, is lined with shops, cafes, and restaurants, offering visitors a chance to explore local artisan goods, indulge in some regional Patagonian delicacies, and relax in the cozy cafés.

Villa La Angostura is an excellent place for nature walks, with numerous trails offering stunning views of the lake and mountains. If you're feeling adventurous, consider taking a short walk along the Bahía Mansa trail, which leads you to a quiet beach where you can enjoy a peaceful moment surrounded by nature.

Los Arrayanes National Park

A visit to Los Arrayanes National Park is one of the main attractions in Villa La Angostura. This park is famous for its Arrayanes trees, which are unique due to their striking white bark and cinnamon-colored trunks. The park is located on the Quetrihué Peninsula, which can be reached by boat or via a scenic hike. The Arrayanes Trail is a 12-kilometer round-trip hike that takes you through a magical forest of these distinctive trees, providing a truly immersive experience in nature. The park also offers an excellent opportunity to spot local wildlife, including birds, deer, and the occasional puma.

A boat ride on Lake Nahuel Huapi is another way to explore the beauty of Los Arrayanes National Park. Several companies offer boat tours from Villa La Angostura to the park, providing guests with the opportunity to take in the magnificent views of the surrounding landscape while learning about the history and ecology of the area.

12.2 Crossing the Andes into Chile

One of the most exciting day trips from Bariloche is crossing the Andes Mountains into Chile. This journey takes you through one of the most scenic routes in Patagonia, offering stunning views of lakes, mountains, and valleys. The crossing is not only an adventure for nature lovers, but also a cultural experience as you get the chance to explore Chilean Patagonia.

The Andean Crossing

The Andean Crossing is a popular route that links Bariloche in Argentina to Puerto Varas in Chile. There are several ways to cross the border, but the most scenic and memorable way is by boat and bus, which is often referred to as the Cruce Andino (Andean Crossing). The trip typically starts with a boat ride across Lake Nahuel Huapi to the port town of Puerto Blest, located in Argentina. From there, passengers take a bus to Lake Frías, where another boat ride takes you across this stunning lake to the Chilean side of Patagonia.

The journey offers spectacular views of the Andes, including towering peaks, deep blue lakes, and lush forests. The boat ride across Lake Frías is particularly scenic, as it passes through narrow fjords surrounded by steep mountains, creating a dramatic and unforgettable landscape.

Puerto Varas and the Chilean Patagonia

Once you reach Chile, the journey continues by bus to Puerto Varas, a charming town located on the shores of Lake Llanquihue. The town is famous for its German-style architecture, picturesque setting, and stunning views of the Osorno Volcano. Puerto Varas is an excellent place to explore if you have time, with numerous outdoor activities such as hiking, fishing, and kayaking.

If you're looking for a longer day trip, you can explore the Vicente Pérez Rosales National Park, which is located nearby and offers hiking opportunities, hot springs, and views of glaciers and waterfalls.

The Return to Bariloche

The trip across the Andes and back to Bariloche can be done as a day trip, but many visitors choose to extend their stay in Puerto Varas for a night or two to explore Chilean Patagonia more fully. Regardless of how long you decide to stay, the journey is a unique and unforgettable experience that offers incredible views and an opportunity to cross the Andean mountain range, one of the most iconic landmarks in South America.

12.3 Visiting the Patagonian Lakes Region

The Patagonian Lakes Region is one of the most beautiful and serene parts of Patagonia, offering travelers the chance to explore some of the most stunning lakes and natural landscapes in Argentina and Chile. This region is easily accessible from Bariloche, making it an ideal destination for a day trip to experience the heart of Patagonia's wilderness.

The Lakes of the Region

The Patagonian Lakes Region is home to several pristine lakes, including Nahuel Huapi, Lake Gutiérrez, Lake Moreno, and Lake Mascardi, all of which are located near Bariloche. Each of these lakes has its own unique charm, with crystal-clear waters, surrounded by snow-capped mountains, dense forests, and abundant wildlife.

- **Lake Gutiérrez:** A short drive from Bariloche, Lake Gutiérrez is a peaceful spot with stunning mountain views. It's a great place for kayaking, fishing, or simply relaxing by the shore. The area around the lake is also home to a number of beautiful hiking trails, such as the Cerro Catedral trail, which offers incredible views of the lake and the surrounding mountains.

- **Lake Mascardi:** This is another picturesque lake located to the south of Bariloche, known for its tranquil waters and scenic surroundings. The lake is ideal for boating, fishing, and hiking, and there are a number of campsites and lodges in the area where you can stay overnight. It's also one of the quieter lakes in the region, making it a perfect escape for those looking to get away from the crowds.

- **Lake Moreno:** Situated to the west of Bariloche, Lake Moreno is known for its dramatic views of the Andes. The lake is part of Nahuel Huapi National Park and offers plenty of opportunities for outdoor activities, including hiking, fishing, and boating. The Circuito Chico drive around the lake provides breathtaking views of the surrounding mountains and forests.

Exploring the Patagonian Lakes

The Patagonian Lakes Region is perfect for those looking to enjoy a mix of outdoor adventure and relaxation. Visitors can enjoy activities such as kayaking on the tranquil lakes, hiking through forests and along rivers, or simply exploring the charming small towns that dot the lakeshores. Towns such as Villa La Angostura and San Martín de los Andes are easily accessible from Bariloche and offer a wonderful blend of local culture, shopping, and excellent dining options.

For a more immersive experience, consider taking a boat tour across one of the lakes, which will allow you to appreciate the vastness and serenity of the area. The boat tours often stop at isolated beaches or points of interest, providing guests with a more intimate experience of Patagonia's stunning natural landscapes.

12.4 Exploring the Ruta de los 7 Lagos

The Ruta de los 7 Lagos (Route of the Seven Lakes) is one of the most famous scenic drives in Argentina, and it is a must-do for any visitor to Bariloche. This stunning 107-kilometer stretch of road runs through Nahuel Huapi National Park, connecting Bariloche to Villa La Angostura, and it passes by seven beautiful lakes that showcase the natural beauty of the Argentine Patagonia region.

The Scenic Drive

The Ruta de los 7 Lagos is a popular route for those who want to experience some of the best landscapes in Argentina. The drive itself is an adventure, with numerous opportunities to stop and take in the views. The road winds through dense forests, along the shores of crystal-clear lakes, and past snow-capped mountains. It's an ideal route for those who love photography, as the views change dramatically around every corner.

The Seven Lakes

The Seven Lakes along the route are Lake Nahuel Huapi, Lake Espejo, Lake Correntoso, Lake Escondido, Lake Villarino, Lake Falkner, and Lake Machónico. Each lake has its own distinct charm, with turquoise waters, dense forests, and towering peaks surrounding them. The lakes are perfect for outdoor activities such as hiking, picnicking, and taking a swim in the summer months.

- **Lake Correntoso** is one of the largest and most well-known lakes along the route, famous for its crystal-clear water and stunning views. It's a popular stop for those interested in water sports, such as kayaking and fishing.

- **Lake Escondido** is one of the more secluded lakes, and it's a beautiful spot for a peaceful break along the route. The lake is surrounded by forests and offers opportunities for hiking and wildlife spotting.

Hiking and Outdoor Activities

The Ruta de los 7 Lagos also offers plenty of hiking opportunities. Many of the lakes along the route have established trails that lead to scenic viewpoints, allowing visitors to enjoy the stunning landscape up close. Hiking around the lakes provides the chance to spot local wildlife, including birds, deer, and guanacos, as well as to enjoy the quiet, untouched beauty of Patagonia.

Completing the Drive

The drive can be completed in one day, but many visitors prefer to take their time and stop at each lake to explore, take photographs, or enjoy a picnic. Along the way, there are several campsites and small villages where you can stop for a break, making the journey an enjoyable and leisurely experience.

Bariloche's location in the heart of Patagonia makes it an ideal base for exploring the surrounding natural wonders. From visiting the charming village of Villa La Angostura to crossing the Andes into Chile and exploring the scenic beauty of the Patagonian Lakes Region, Bariloche offers a wide variety of day trips for nature lovers. Whether you're looking to relax by pristine lakes, enjoy panoramic views, or immerse yourself in the region's rugged landscapes, these day trips provide unforgettable experiences that allow you to experience the best of Patagonia.

Chapter 13: Travel Tips for Visiting Bariloche

Bariloche, a scenic gem nestled in Argentina's Patagonia region, offers visitors an unforgettable experience with its breathtaking landscapes, outdoor activities, and unique culture. Whether you are a first-time traveler or a seasoned adventurer, knowing some essential travel tips can help make your visit to Bariloche smoother and more enjoyable. This chapter covers important advice on currency, language, safety, health, local culture, and packing for your trip. By the end, you will be prepared to make the most of your time in this beautiful Patagonian city.

13.1 Currency, Language, and Communication

When traveling to Bariloche, understanding the local currency, language, and communication methods is essential for navigating the city comfortably. While Argentina has its own unique customs, Bariloche is a popular tourist destination, so it's relatively easy to interact with locals and access services.

Currency: Argentine Peso (ARS)

The official currency in Argentina is the Argentine Peso (ARS). It's important to note that credit cards are widely accepted in most hotels, restaurants, and stores, but having cash on hand is still advisable, especially when traveling to smaller towns or for minor expenses like tips and small purchases.

- **ATMs and Currency Exchange:** ATMs are available in Bariloche, and many of them offer cash withdrawals in Argentine pesos. However, you may find that the withdrawal fees are high, especially for international cards. Currency exchange services are available in the city, particularly at banks or specialized exchange offices called "casas de cambio". It's a good idea to compare rates to ensure you get the best exchange rate.

- **Cash and Tipping:** While most major establishments accept credit cards, it's recommended to carry cash for smaller purchases or when visiting remote areas. Tipping in Argentina is customary, and it's usually expected in restaurants, taxis, and other service industries. A 10% tip is standard in restaurants if the service charge is not included in the bill.

Language: Spanish

The official language in Bariloche is Spanish, and it's the most widely spoken language across Argentina. While many people in Bariloche, especially in the tourism industry, speak English, learning a few key phrases in Spanish can go a long way in enhancing your experience.

Some useful Spanish phrases for travelers include:

- **Hola, ¿cómo estás?** (Hello, how are you?)

- **¿Cuánto cuesta?** (How much does it cost?)

- **¿Dónde está el baño?** (Where is the bathroom?)

- **Por favor** (Please)

- **Gracias** (Thank you)

- **¿Habla inglés?** (Do you speak English?)

If you are venturing outside of Bariloche to smaller, more rural areas, it may be harder to find English speakers, so knowing basic Spanish phrases can be quite helpful.

Communication: Wi-Fi and Phone Use

Bariloche has a decent level of infrastructure, and most hotels, cafes, and restaurants offer free Wi-Fi for customers. However, depending on the area you are in, the signal might not always be as strong, especially if you venture into remote locations or the surrounding mountains.

- **SIM Cards and Mobile Phones:** If you need a local phone number, it's easy to purchase a SIM card from one of Argentina's mobile service providers (Personal, Movistar, Claro) at kiosks or stores in the city. These SIM cards offer prepaid plans for data, calls, and texting. Ensure that your phone is unlocked and compatible with Argentine networks before purchasing a local SIM.

- **Emergency Numbers:** In case of emergencies, the general emergency number in Argentina is 911 for police, fire, and medical emergencies.

13.2 Safety and Health Recommendations

Bariloche is generally a safe destination for tourists, but like any popular tourist location, it's important to remain aware of your surroundings and take basic safety precautions. Additionally, being mindful of your health while traveling ensures that your trip remains enjoyable.

Safety Tips

- **Crime and Petty Theft:** As in many tourist destinations, Bariloche is not immune to petty theft, such as pickpocketing. To protect yourself, avoid displaying large amounts of cash or valuables in public. When exploring the city or participating in outdoor activities, keep your belongings secure, especially in crowded areas like markets, bus stations, or tourist attractions.

- **Safety in Remote Areas:** If you're planning on hiking, exploring forests, or traveling to more remote areas, always let someone know your itinerary. Many trails in the surrounding mountains can be challenging, so it's advisable to go with a guide or at least a partner. Weather conditions can change rapidly, especially in winter, so always check the forecast before heading out and ensure you're prepared for the elements.

- **Wildlife Encounters:** While wildlife sightings are a thrilling part of Bariloche's outdoor experience, it's important to exercise caution when encountering wild animals. Keep a safe distance from animals, especially larger ones like pumas or wild boar. If you're trekking, be aware of the animals that inhabit the area and follow safety guidelines provided by tour guides or park authorities.

Health Recommendations

- **Medical Services:** Bariloche has modern medical facilities, including hospitals and pharmacies, that can cater to most health needs. Sanatorio San Carlos and Hospital Zonal de Bariloche are two major medical centers in the city, with English-speaking staff available at some points. Many pharmacies also offer over-the-counter medication for minor ailments like headaches or stomach issues.

- **Travel Insurance:** It's highly recommended to have travel insurance that covers medical expenses, especially if you plan on engaging in outdoor activities such as hiking, skiing, or paragliding. Make sure your insurance includes coverage for emergency evacuation in case of a serious injury or illness.

- **Vaccinations and Health Precautions:** There are no mandatory vaccinations for travelers to Argentina, but it's a good idea to check with your healthcare provider for any recommended vaccinations based on your health history and travel plans. The most common vaccinations include those for hepatitis A, hepatitis B, and typhoid. If you plan on traveling to rural areas or engaging in outdoor activities, make sure to bring sunscreen, insect repellent, and a first-aid kit.

- **Water Safety:** Tap water in Bariloche is safe to drink, as the city receives its water from pure mountain sources. However, if you're traveling to remote areas, it's advisable to drink bottled water or boil water before consuming it.

13.3 Navigating the Local Culture and Etiquette

Understanding and respecting local culture and etiquette can make your time in Bariloche more enjoyable and help you build positive relationships with locals. Argentine culture is warm, friendly, and welcoming, and locals are often eager to share their knowledge of the region with visitors.

Social Etiquette

- **Greetings:** In Argentina, it's customary to greet people with a friendly "Hola" (hello) or "Buenos días" (good morning) when meeting them. Argentine people are known for their warmth, so don't be surprised if you are greeted with a hug or a cheek kiss if you become familiar with someone. However, for more formal or professional settings, a handshake is still common.

- **Dining Etiquette:** The meal schedule in Argentina is different from many other countries. Lunch is typically served from 1:00 PM to 3:00 PM, and dinner often starts around 9:00 PM or later, especially on weekends. When dining in restaurants, it's customary to wait for everyone to be served before starting to eat. Argentinians are known for their love of asado (barbecue), and sharing meals with family and friends is an important social activity. If invited to someone's home, it's polite to bring a small gift, such as wine or dessert.

- **Tipping:** Tipping in Argentina is generally appreciated, especially in the service industry. While it's not as obligatory as in some countries, a 10% tip is customary in restaurants if the service charge is not already included in the bill. For taxis, rounding up the fare is appreciated, while hotel staff may be tipped for luggage assistance.

- **Time Sensitivity:** Argentinians tend to have a more relaxed approach to time, so punctuality isn't always expected, especially in social situations. However, if you are attending a formal event or meeting a business associate, it's best to arrive on time. In restaurants and bars, service may be slower than in some other countries, but this is a cultural difference that adds to the relaxed atmosphere of the dining experience.

Cultural Sensitivities

- **Respect for Local Traditions:** Bariloche, like much of Argentina, has a rich indigenous history, and it's important to respect the cultures and traditions of the region's indigenous groups, particularly the Mapuche people, who have lived in Patagonia for centuries. Visitors should be mindful of the area's indigenous heritage, especially when visiting cultural sites or engaging in activities related to the environment.

- **Dress Code:** The dress code in Bariloche is generally casual, with outdoor clothing being most appropriate for daily activities. Comfortable shoes are essential for exploring the city and hiking, and you'll want to dress in layers, especially if you're visiting during the colder months. While more formal attire is required for fine dining or upscale venues, the majority of Bariloche's casual and outdoor activities allow for a relaxed dress code.

Local Food and Drink Etiquette

- **Mate:** The national drink of Argentina is mate (pronounced MAH-teh), a herbal tea made from the leaves of the yerba mate plant. It is often served in a gourd with a metal straw. Sharing mate is a social activity, and if someone offers you a drink, it's considered impolite to refuse. If you're unfamiliar with mate, it's customary to drink the entire portion when offered and then return the gourd to the person offering it, signaling that you're done. Be aware that mate is enjoyed throughout the day, but it's most commonly consumed in the morning or afternoon.

- **Asado (Barbecue):** Asado, or Argentine barbecue, is a beloved cultural tradition, and many families and groups gather to enjoy this hearty meal. If you're invited to an asado, it's customary to bring something, such as a bottle of wine or dessert. The meat is typically served with side dishes such as ensalada rusa (potato salad) and papas fritas (fries), and meals are often accompanied by long conversations and good company.

13.4 Essential Packing Tips

When visiting Bariloche, packing smartly for the region's varied climate and outdoor activities is key to having a comfortable and enjoyable trip. Patagonia's weather can be unpredictable, so it's important to be prepared for changing conditions. Below are some essential packing tips to ensure you're ready for everything Bariloche has to offer.

Clothing for All Seasons

- **Layering is Key:** The weather in Bariloche can fluctuate dramatically, especially during the transitional seasons of fall and spring. Be sure to pack clothing that can be layered, including lightweight base layers, a warm fleece or jacket, and a waterproof outer layer. Even in summer, temperatures can drop quickly in the evenings, so it's important to have layers that can be added or removed as needed.

- **Waterproof Gear:** Whether you're hiking through the forests or exploring the lakes, it's important to bring waterproof gear. A good-quality rain jacket, waterproof boots, and an umbrella are all essential for dealing with the occasional rain showers that occur throughout the year.

- **Winter Clothing:** If you're visiting Bariloche in winter, especially if you plan to ski or engage in other winter sports, make sure to pack warm clothing such as thermal undergarments, a heavy-duty jacket, gloves, a hat, and scarves. Bariloche can get quite cold in the winter, with snow and freezing temperatures common in higher altitudes.

Outdoor Equipment

- **Hiking Boots:** Comfortable, sturdy, and waterproof hiking boots are essential if you plan on exploring Bariloche's hiking trails. The terrain can be rugged, and having proper footwear will make your hikes more enjoyable and safe.

- **Sunscreen and Sunglasses:** Even in cooler weather, Patagonia's high-altitude sun can be intense. Pack sunscreen with a high SPF and a good pair of sunglasses to protect your eyes from UV rays, especially during outdoor activities like hiking, kayaking, or skiing.

Miscellaneous

- **Camera:** Bariloche is a photographer's paradise, so don't forget to bring a camera with extra memory cards and batteries to capture the stunning landscapes and wildlife.

- **Travel Adapter:** Argentina uses Type C and Type I power outlets, so you'll need a plug adapter for your electronic devices. The voltage is 220V, so check that your devices are compatible or bring a voltage converter if necessary.

- **Medications and First Aid Kit:** Bring any necessary medications with you, as pharmacies in Bariloche may not carry specific items you use regularly. It's also a good idea to have a small first aid kit with basics such as band-aids, antiseptic cream, and any personal health items you may need.

With these travel tips, you'll be well-prepared for your visit to Bariloche. Understanding the local currency, language, and communication methods, being aware of safety and health recommendations, respecting the local culture and etiquette, and packing smartly for Patagonia's unpredictable weather will help ensure that your trip is enjoyable and stress-free. Bariloche offers a remarkable experience, and with these tips in hand, you'll be ready to embrace everything this breathtaking destination has to offer.

Chapter 14: Sustainable Travel in Bariloche

As one of Argentina's most beautiful and sought-after destinations, Bariloche offers travelers the chance to explore pristine landscapes, magnificent lakes, and towering mountains. However, with the growing popularity of the region as a tourist destination, the responsibility of protecting its natural and cultural heritage has become ever more important. Sustainable travel, or eco-tourism, has become a critical part of the tourism industry in Bariloche. This chapter focuses on how travelers can minimize their environmental footprint, support local communities, and contribute to preserving the natural beauty of this Patagonian paradise.

In the following sections, we will explore the concept of eco-tourism and responsible travel, how to support local communities and businesses, and the importance of preserving the natural environment while enjoying all that Bariloche has to offer.

14.1 Eco-Tourism and Responsible Travel

Eco-tourism, or sustainable tourism, is about traveling in a way that respects the environment and local cultures while promoting the conservation of natural resources. In Bariloche, eco-tourism has gained traction over the years, with many businesses, organizations, and local authorities working towards maintaining the delicate balance between tourism and environmental conservation.

What is Eco-Tourism?

Eco-tourism emphasizes environmental sustainability by encouraging low-impact travel experiences, minimizing waste, and ensuring that the local ecosystems and wildlife are respected. It is about enjoying nature and supporting conservation efforts while having minimal negative effects on the environment. In Bariloche, eco-tourism also includes cultural sustainability, ensuring that local traditions and lifestyles are preserved while benefiting from tourism.

Responsible travel goes beyond eco-tourism—it involves travelers making conscious choices that reduce their environmental impact, conserve resources, and contribute to the local economy. In Bariloche, eco-friendly travel can be practiced in several ways, from choosing sustainable accommodations to participating in activities that promote environmental stewardship.

Eco-Friendly Accommodation

Many accommodations in Bariloche are embracing eco-friendly practices such as energy efficiency, water conservation, and waste reduction. Staying at an eco-conscious hotel or lodge allows you to reduce your carbon footprint while still enjoying comfort and hospitality.

- **Sustainable Lodging:** Eco-lodges and boutique hotels in Bariloche often have sustainability certifications, which include practices such as using renewable energy, recycling, and employing water-saving technologies. Many also promote the use of local products, such as organic foods and locally made toiletries, which supports the region's economy and reduces transportation emissions.

- **Green Certifications:** When selecting accommodation, look for businesses that have green certifications or participate in programs like Green Key or EarthCheck. These certifications signify that the hotel or lodge adheres to high environmental standards, such as waste reduction, energy efficiency, and responsible resource management.

- **Off-the-Grid Stays:** For the more adventurous eco-travelers, some remote cabins and lodges in Bariloche offer off-the-grid experiences. These eco-lodges are typically powered by solar energy and often feature composting toilets, natural water systems, and minimal environmental impact, offering an authentic and sustainable stay in nature.

Eco-Tourism Activities

Bariloche offers an abundance of eco-tourism activities that allow visitors to enjoy the region's beauty while promoting environmental conservation. The focus is on experiencing nature without disrupting its delicate ecosystems. Here are a few popular eco-friendly activities:

- **Hiking and Trekking:** Bariloche is famous for its hiking trails, many of which are located in Nahuel Huapi National Park and Los Alerces National Park. These trails allow visitors to explore the region's forests, lakes, and mountains while minimizing their environmental impact. As you hike, ensure that you stay on designated paths to avoid disturbing the native flora and fauna.

- **Kayaking and Canoeing:** Exploring Bariloche's pristine lakes, such as Lake Nahuel Huapi, by kayak or canoe is an excellent way to enjoy the environment while minimizing your environmental footprint. Kayaking allows you to silently paddle through the clear waters and observe wildlife without creating pollution or noise.

- **Wildlife Watching:** Bariloche is home to many wildlife species, including Andean condors, huemul deer, and Magellanic woodpeckers. Responsible wildlife watching means observing animals from a safe distance without disturbing their habitats. Eco-tourism guides often emphasize the importance of not feeding wildlife and maintaining quiet to avoid causing stress to the animals.

- **Bird Watching:** Birdwatching is a peaceful and educational eco-tourism activity that allows visitors to connect with nature while minimizing environmental disruption. Bariloche is home to a diverse array of bird species, and many tour companies offer guided birdwatching trips, ensuring that visitors are respectful of the environment and adhere to responsible observation practices.

Carbon Offset Programs

As an eco-conscious traveler, you can offset the carbon emissions generated by your travel, including flights and other transportation. Many travel companies in Bariloche are involved in carbon offset programs, where a portion of your travel fee goes toward projects that reduce greenhouse gases or promote environmental restoration. These programs often focus on reforestation projects or clean energy initiatives. Inquire with your tour operators about whether they offer carbon offset options and consider participating to help minimize your impact on the environment.

14.2 Supporting Local Communities and Businesses

Responsible travel goes beyond minimizing environmental impacts—it also involves supporting local communities and ensuring that tourism benefits those who live and work in the region. In Bariloche, many small businesses and artisans rely on tourism to sustain their livelihoods, and supporting them can make a significant positive impact.

Buying Local Products

One of the best ways to support local businesses in Bariloche is by purchasing locally made products. The city is famous for its high-quality chocolates, craft beers, and artisan goods. By buying these products, you're not only supporting the local economy, but you're also ensuring that traditional crafts and industries continue to thrive.

- **Chocolates and Sweets:** Bariloche is often referred to as the "chocolate capital" of Argentina, and for good reason. The city boasts numerous artisan chocolate shops that produce handcrafted sweets made from the finest ingredients. Buying chocolate from local stores like Rapa Nui, Mamuschka, and Del Turista helps support these

131

businesses and promotes sustainable production practices.

- **Craft Beer and Wines:** Patagonia is known for its craft beer scene, with many breweries producing high-quality beer using locally sourced ingredients. Support local breweries by purchasing their products from bars, restaurants, or retail stores. Likewise, Argentina's wine regions, including those near Bariloche, produce excellent wines that support local agriculture and vineyards.

- **Handmade Artisanal Goods:** Local artisans in Bariloche create beautiful handmade items such as wooden sculptures, leather goods, woven textiles, and silver jewelry. These goods represent the region's cultural heritage and offer a great way to take home a piece of Patagonia while supporting local craftsmanship.

Supporting Eco-Conscious Tour Operators

When choosing a tour operator for outdoor activities, prioritize those who are committed to sustainability and responsible travel. Many eco-conscious tour companies in Bariloche focus on minimizing their environmental impact by using eco-friendly equipment, following Leave No Trace principles, and supporting local conservation efforts.

Some companies also work directly with local communities to ensure that tourism provides economic benefits without negatively impacting indigenous traditions or local cultures. By choosing these operators, you help ensure that tourism continues to support the local economy while promoting environmental and cultural conservation.

Volunteering and Community Involvement

Volunteering during your trip to Bariloche can be a rewarding way to engage with the local community and contribute to meaningful projects. Many organizations in Bariloche, such as environmental NGOs or social initiatives, welcome volunteers who want to help protect the environment or support community-based programs. Volunteering gives you the opportunity to experience the local culture in a deeper way and make a positive impact during your visit.

14.3 Preserving the Natural Environment

Bariloche is blessed with some of the most beautiful and pristine natural environments in the world. However, the region is facing increasing pressures from tourism, including habitat degradation, littering, and resource overuse. As a traveler, it's essential to be mindful of your environmental footprint and take steps to preserve the natural beauty of Bariloche for future generations.

Leave No Trace Principles

When exploring the outdoors, it's important to follow the Leave No Trace (LNT) principles. These guidelines promote minimizing your environmental impact by leaving nature as you found it. LNT principles include:

- **Plan ahead and prepare:** Know the weather conditions, required equipment, and regulations before embarking on outdoor activities such as hiking, kayaking, or camping.

- **Travel and camp on durable surfaces:** Stick to designated trails, campsites, and paths to avoid disturbing fragile ecosystems. Avoid creating new trails or shortcuts, and always camp in established areas.

- **Dispose of waste properly:** Always carry out all trash, including biodegradable items like food scraps, and dispose of waste in proper facilities. Pack out everything you bring with you, including cigarette butts and toilet paper.

- **Leave what you find:** Do not pick plants, disturb wildlife, or remove rocks or other natural features. Take only photographs and leave the environment as you found it.

- **Respect wildlife:** Observe animals from a distance without disturbing them or their habitats. Avoid feeding wildlife, as it can alter their behavior and lead to problems.

Reducing Plastic Use

One of the most significant contributors to environmental damage around the world is plastic waste. In Bariloche, many businesses and local organizations are working hard to reduce single-use plastic, and as a responsible traveler, you can play your part.

- **Reusable Water Bottles:** Rather than buying bottled water, bring a reusable water bottle with you. Bariloche has excellent tap water, which is clean and safe to drink, so refilling your bottle at water stations or your accommodation is an easy and sustainable option.

- **Avoid Plastic Bags:** Many stores and markets in Bariloche now offer alternatives to plastic bags, such as cloth bags or paper bags. Carry your own reusable shopping bag to reduce plastic consumption.

Supporting Conservation Efforts

If you're passionate about preserving the environment, consider donating to or participating in conservation efforts during your visit to Bariloche. Many local organizations focus on environmental preservation, such as wildlife protection programs and habitat restoration projects. These organizations often rely on donations and volunteers to help protect the natural areas that make Bariloche such a unique and beautiful destination.

- **Nahuel Huapi Foundation:** The Fundación Nahuel Huapi is an NGO dedicated to the preservation of the Nahuel Huapi National Park, its ecosystems, and biodiversity. They focus on educating the public, protecting wildlife habitats, and conducting research to support conservation efforts.

- **Wildlife Monitoring Projects:** Some companies and organizations in Bariloche offer wildlife monitoring programs that contribute to protecting native species, such as the huemul deer and the Andean condor. By participating in these programs, you can directly contribute to the protection of Patagonia's endangered wildlife.

Sustainable travel in Bariloche is about making conscious choices that minimize your environmental impact, support local communities, and preserve the beauty of Patagonia for future generations. By practicing eco-tourism, supporting local businesses, and following the principles of conservation, you can enjoy all the wonders that Bariloche has to offer while contributing to its long-term preservation.

Chapter 15: Conclusion and Final Thoughts

Bariloche is undoubtedly one of Argentina's most iconic destinations, attracting visitors from around the world with its natural beauty, outdoor adventures, and cultural experiences. Whether you're looking to explore majestic mountains, pristine lakes, or indulge in the local cuisine, Bariloche offers something for every traveler. From eco-tourism enthusiasts to adrenaline junkies, families, and culture seekers, Bariloche provides an unparalleled travel experience. This final chapter will reflect on why Bariloche is a must-visit destination, offer a quick guide to planning your trip, and provide useful resources to ensure your visit is as smooth as possible.

15.1 Why Bariloche is a Must-Visit Destination

Bariloche has earned its reputation as one of Argentina's most popular and breathtaking destinations, drawing travelers from around the globe. But what makes this Patagonian town so irresistible? Here are some compelling reasons why Bariloche should be on every traveler's bucket list.

1. Stunning Natural Beauty

The first reason Bariloche stands out is its unparalleled natural beauty. Nestled on the shores of Nahuel Huapi Lake and surrounded by the majestic Andes Mountains, the landscape in Bariloche is nothing short of spectacular. From the glacial lakes to the lush forests, rugged hills, and snow-capped peaks, every corner of Bariloche offers a picture-perfect scene. Whether you're hiking through ancient forests, kayaking across crystal-clear lakes, or simply taking in the views from the Cerro Campanario, Bariloche is a paradise for nature lovers and photographers alike.

2. Outdoor Adventure and Activities

Bariloche is known for its abundance of outdoor activities that cater to all types of adventurers. In the winter, Cerro Catedral becomes a haven for skiers and snowboarders, while in the warmer months, the region transforms into a paradise for hikers, mountain bikers, kayakers, and wildlife enthusiasts. Whether you're trekking through national parks, paragliding over the Andes, fishing in crystal-clear rivers, or enjoying the many water sports on Lake Nahuel Huapi, Bariloche offers thrilling experiences for anyone who loves outdoor adventure.

3. Rich Cultural Heritage

In addition to its natural beauty, Bariloche boasts a vibrant cultural heritage that reflects the diverse influences of its indigenous communities and European settlers. The town's Swiss and German roots are reflected in its alpine-style architecture, local cuisine (including world-renowned chocolates), and traditional festivals like the Fiesta Nacional de la Nieve. Bariloche's museums, art galleries, and theaters offer an enriching experience for visitors who want to delve deeper into the region's history and culture.

4. A Destination for All Seasons

Bariloche is a year-round destination, offering different experiences depending on the season. In the winter months, the snow-covered landscape provides the perfect setting for skiing, snowboarding, and cozying up in mountain lodges. In the summer, Bariloche's lakes and forests offer perfect conditions for hiking, fishing, and enjoying the outdoors. The varied seasons ensure that there is always something exciting to do in Bariloche, no matter when you visit.

5. Delicious Local Cuisine

The culinary scene in Bariloche is one of the most delightful aspects of the region. Known for its chocolate, Bariloche has earned the title of Argentina's "chocolate capital." Visitors can indulge in handcrafted chocolates from the city's many chocolate shops, as well as savor traditional Argentine dishes such as asado (barbecue), empanadas, and patagonian lamb. Pair your meals with locally produced wines or craft beers, and you'll find that Bariloche's food scene is an experience in itself.

6. Accessibility and Local Infrastructure

Despite its remote location in Patagonia, Bariloche is easily accessible, with a modern airport connecting it to major Argentine cities like Buenos Aires, Cordoba, and Mendoza. The city is well-equipped with services for tourists, from restaurants and accommodations to tour companies and transportation options. Whether you're arriving by plane, bus, or car, getting to Bariloche is simple, and once you're there, you'll find plenty of facilities to make your stay comfortable.

15.2 Planning Your Trip: A Quick Guide

Planning your trip to Bariloche doesn't need to be overwhelming. With a little preparation, you can make the most of your time in this stunning destination. Here's a quick guide to help you plan your visit.

1. When to Visit

The best time to visit Bariloche depends on the activities you want to do:

- **Summer (December to February):** This is the peak season in Bariloche, particularly for outdoor activities like hiking, kayaking, and cycling. The weather is mild, and the days are long, making it perfect for exploring the natural surroundings. Keep in mind that this is also the most crowded time, so it's best to book accommodations and activities in advance.

- **Winter (June to August):** If skiing or snowboarding is on your itinerary, winter is the best time to visit. Bariloche's **Cerro Catedral** is one of the largest ski resorts in South America, attracting snow sports enthusiasts from around the world. Winter in Bariloche also offers opportunities for snowshoeing, snowmobiling, and cozy nights by the fire.

- **Fall (March to May) and Spring (September to November):** These shoulder seasons offer a more peaceful experience with fewer tourists, lower prices, and still plenty of outdoor activities. Fall, in particular, is beautiful, as the forests around Bariloche turn vibrant shades of red, orange, and yellow.

2. How to Get There

- **By Air:** Bariloche has its own international airport, San Carlos de Bariloche Airport (BRC), which is around 13 kilometers from the city center. Flights from Buenos Aires and other major cities in Argentina are frequent and convenient. If you're coming from abroad, you may need to connect through Buenos Aires, which is a major hub.

- **By Bus:** If you prefer traveling overland, Bariloche is accessible by bus from Buenos Aires and other major cities. The journey from Buenos Aires takes about 20 hours, and buses are comfortable with amenities such as Wi-Fi, reclining seats, and meals.

- **By Car:** Renting a car is a great option if you want flexibility to explore the region at your own pace. Bariloche is well-connected by road, and the surrounding landscapes make for stunning drives. The Ruta 40 (Route 40) is one of the most scenic roads in Argentina, offering an unforgettable road trip experience.

3. Where to Stay

Bariloche offers a wide variety of accommodations to suit every budget and preference. From luxury resorts with panoramic views of the lakes to more affordable hostels and cozy cabins, there is something for everyone. Popular areas to stay include the Civic Center for easy access to shops, restaurants, and cultural attractions, as well as Llao Llao for a more tranquil lakeside experience. Book accommodations in advance, especially if you're traveling during peak season.

4. What to Pack

- **Clothing:** Patagonia's weather is unpredictable, so it's important to pack for all seasons. In addition to comfortable clothing for outdoor activities (hiking boots, lightweight jackets), be sure to bring layers for colder weather, especially if visiting in the winter.

- **Sun Protection:** The sun in Patagonia can be intense, so bring sunglasses, sunscreen, and a hat to protect your skin.

- **Gear:** If you plan to do outdoor activities such as hiking or kayaking, bring appropriate gear like a backpack, water bottle, and a camera. Some activities, like skiing, may require renting equipment, so check with tour operators in advance.

5. Getting Around Bariloche

Bariloche is a small city, and most of the main attractions are easily accessible by foot or by public transportation. The city also has affordable taxi services. If you're planning to explore the surrounding national parks or nearby villages, consider renting a car or booking guided tours for convenience.

15.3 Resources and Useful Contacts

Having reliable resources and contacts can make your trip to Bariloche even easier. Here's a list of useful contacts and online resources to help you during your travels:

1. Tourism Information Centers

- **Bariloche Tourism Office:** Located in the city center, this office provides maps, brochures, and useful information about activities, accommodations, and events. The staff speaks multiple languages, including English.

  - **Address:** Mitre 535, Bariloche

  - **Phone:** +54 294 442 1133

  - **Website:** barilocheturismo.gob.ar

2. Guided Tours and Adventure Companies

- **Bariloche Adventure:** Specializes in outdoor adventure tours, including hiking, kayaking, fishing, and skiing.

- **Catedral Alta Patagonia:** This company runs Cerro Catedral ski resort and offers snow sports, equipment rentals, and guided skiing tours.

- **Wildlife Patagonia:** Offers wildlife-focused tours, including birdwatching, wildlife safaris, and eco-tours of Bariloche and its surrounding areas.

3. Transportation Providers

- **La Agencia Bariloche:** Provides car rentals, private transfers, and shuttle services to and from the airport.

- **Andesmar:** Offers long-distance bus services from Bariloche to Buenos Aires and other Argentine cities.

4. Emergency Contacts

- **Police (Policía):** 101

- **Medical Emergencies (Emergencias Médicas):** 107

- **Fire Department (Bomberos):** 100

Bariloche is a remarkable destination for travelers seeking adventure, relaxation, and a deep connection with nature. Its stunning landscapes, outdoor activities, rich culture, and vibrant community make it one of Argentina's must-visit places. Whether you're trekking in national parks, savoring the world-class chocolates, or enjoying the peaceful serenity of Patagonia's lakes, Bariloche has something for every kind of traveler.

By planning your trip thoughtfully—taking into account the best times to visit, knowing how to get around, supporting local businesses, and packing appropriately—you'll be well-equipped to experience the best that Bariloche has to offer. Don't forget to embrace the local culture, respect the natural environment, and make lasting memories in this stunning corner of Argentina.

146

Printed in Great Britain
by Amazon